D0388646

DYLAN MARLAIS THOMAS was born in Swansea on 27 October 1914. After leaving school he worked briefly as a junior reporter on the *South Wales Evening Post* before embarking on a literary career in London. Here he rapidly established himself as one of the finest poets of his generation. *Eighteen Poems* appeared in 1934, *Twenty-five Poems* in 1936, and *Deaths and Entrances* in 1946; his *Collected Poems* were published in 1952. Throughout his life Thomas wrote short stories, his most famous collection being *Portrait of the Artist as a Young Dog*. He also wrote filmscripts, broadcast stories and talks, lectured in America, and wrote the radio play *Under Milk Wood*. On 9 November 1953, shortly after his thirty-ninth birthday, he collapsed and died in New York. His body is buried in Laugharne, Wales, his home for many years.

DANIEL JONES knew Dylan Thomas all his life and is the author of *My Friend Dylan Thomas* (Dent 1977). He also edited *The Poems* which contains almost all of Dylan Thomas's poetry.

DYLAN THOMAS'
BOAT HOUSE
LAUGHARNE DYFED WALES TEL:

DYLAN THOMAS

Under Milk Wood

A PLAY FOR VOICES

Prefaces (1954 and 1974) by Daniel Jones

J.M. Dent & Sons Ltd: London
EVERYMAN'S LIBRARY

Under Milk Wood was first broadcast by the BBC on 25 January 1954. It was presented on the stage in the tenth Edinburgh Festival in 1956 and extracts from it were shown on BBC television. The stage production, by Douglas Cleverdon and Edward Burnham, of the play was given at the New (now Albery) Theatre, London, in 1956. The film of the play, which opened the Venice Festival in 1971, was released in 1972 with screenplay by Andrew Sinclair and starring Richard Burton and Peter O'Toole.

The cast list of the first broadcast is reproduced on pp. 93–4 of this volume.

Preface

On the 9th of November 1953, a few days after his
thirty-ninth birthday, Dylan Thomas died in New York. At
the time of his death a new poem was still unfinished, and
the collaboration with Stravinsky, planned for the end of
the year, had not even begun. The survival of *Under Milk
Wood* is a remarkable piece of good fortune, for it was not
completed until Thomas came within a month of his death,
though he had worked intermittently on the play for nearly
ten years. There was no time for any final revision of the
text by the poet himself, but we are justified in regarding
what he has left as a complete work.

The publication of Thomas's *Collected Poems* in 1952
marked the end of one period of his literary development;
after this, according to his own words, he intended to
turn from the strictly personal kind of poetry to a more
public form of expression, and to large-scale dramatic
works in particular, where there would be scope for all
his versatility, for his gifts of humour and characterization
as well as his genius for poetry. It is fortunate that at least
one of these projected works has been preserved for us.

Under Milk Wood, a Play for Voices grew by a slow and
natural process, and the story of that growth, known only
to a few friends of the poet, is most interesting. Thomas
liked small towns by the sea best, and small Welsh towns
by the sea best of all. Before the war he lived for many
years in Laugharne, and during the war for a time in New
Quay; there is no doubt that he absorbed the spirit of these

places and, through imagination and insight, the spirit of all other places like them. When, more than ten years ago, a short talk was commissioned by the BBC, the description of a small Welsh seaside town was a natural choice of subject. *Quite Early One Morning,* short as it is, and written so many years ago, is closely related to *Under Milk Wood.* There is the same sequence of 'ime, though limited to the morning hours and in winter, not spring; we hear the dreams of the sleeping town and see the sleepers getting up and going about their business. Captain Tiny Evans and the Rev. Thomas Evans are pygmies beside the blind sea-captain and the reverend bard of Llareggub, but Miss Hughes 'The Cosy' recalls Myfanwy Price, Manchester House stands ready for Mog Edwards, and the husbands of Mrs Ogmore-Pritchard are already at their tasks: 'Dust the china, feed the canary, sweep the drawing-room floor; and before you let the sun in, mind he wipes his shoes.'

The success of this broadcast talk suggested to Thomas a more extended work against the same kind of background. At first he was unable to decide upon the form of the work, and there was much discussion with friends about a stage play, a comedy in verse, and a radio play with a blind man as narrator and central character. The blind man, a natural bridge between eye and ear for the radio listener, survives in *Under Milk Wood,* with the difference that Captain Cat is made to share his central position with two anonymous narrators. But the simple time sequence of *Quite Early One Morning,* which resembles the pattern of *Under Milk Wood* so closely, at first appeared inadequate; some kind of plot seemed to be necessary. Thomas thought he had found the theme he wanted in the contrast between the mythical town and the surrounding world, the conflict between the eccentrics, strong in their individuality and freedom, and the sane ones who sacrifice everything to some notion of conformity. The whole population cannot very well be accommodated inside the walls of a lunatic asylum; so the sane world decrees that the town itself shall be declared an 'insane area', with all traffic and goods diverted from it. Captain Cat, spokesman of the indignant citizens, insists that the sanity of the town should be put on trial in the town hall with every legal formality; he will be Counsel for the Defence and the citizens themselves will be witnesses. The trial takes place, but it comes to a surprising end. The final speech for the Prosecution consists of a full and minute description of the ideally sane town; as soon as they hear this, the people withdraw their defence and beg to be cordoned off from the sane world as soon as possible.

Once more settled in his house overlooking Laugharne Estuary, Thomas began working according to the plan of *The Town Was Mad,* as he called it, and brought the action up to the delivery of letters by Willy Nilly the postman; but by that time he had changed his mind, and there was no letter for Captain Cat about the sanity or the insanity of the town. When this first part of *Under Milk Wood,* with the provisional title *Llareggub, a Piece for Radio Perhaps,* appeared for the first time in *Botteghe Oscure,*[1] Thomas had returned to the plan of *Quite Early One Morning*; his intention was to limit the picture to the town itself, with hardly a suggestion of a world beyond the town, and to extend the time sequence to form a complete cycle.

Before Thomas's third visit to the USA in 1953, the title *Under Milk Wood, a Play for Voices* was decided upon, the first part, *Llareggub,* was revised, and the work had been extended to the end of Polly Garter's song, where it first appears. In this form the play was read at the Kaufmann Auditorium of the Young Men's Hebrew

[1] *Quaderno IX,* edited by Marguerite Caetani (Rome, 1952).

Association on the 15th and the 29th of May; the poet himself read the parts of the First Voice and the Rev. Eli Jenkins.

As soon as Thomas returned to Britain the BBC urged him to complete the work without further delay, and, by omitting some projected ballads and unfinished material for the closing section, he was able to supply a finished version at the end of October. The first broadcast of the whole work, produced by Douglas Cleverdon with a distinguished all Welsh cast, was given on the 25th of January 1954, with a repetition two days later.

In case *Under Milk Wood* falls into the hands of a Welsh philologist, it must be made clear that the language used is Anglo-Welsh. Dylan Thomas spoke no Welsh, and the reader must imitate his inconsistency if he wishes to hear the words as they were pronounced by the poet himself. A note on pronunciation will be found at the end of the book.

January 1954   DANIEL JONES

Second Preface

Twenty years have passed since I wrote the first Preface to *Under Milk Wood*, and in the course of that time the play has proved its enduring quality. It has been read privately, read publicly, staged and translated into many languages. In my view, the fame of Dylan Thomas will rest ultimately on a handful of poems; but, in the meantime, *Under Milk Wood* is surely his most widely known composition. Many who have read the play or heard it read many times are afraid to face any other work of Dylan Thomas, except perhaps the apparently straightforward stories of *Portrait of the Artist as a Young Dog* and one or two radio scripts.

This fear is not altogether unreasonable. Thomas's work inhabits two different worlds: the private, introspective world of his most concentrated and meticulously constructed poems, and the public, extrovert world of his broadly humorous and highly coloured 'prose'. *Under Milk Wood* belongs in the main to the second world, in which Thomas was guided to some extent by professional opportunism, and purposely aimed at immediate effect and accessibility. This does not lessen the quality of the play. Thomas would have failed in his professionalism if he had not recognized that in this medium, unlike the 'private' medium of a poem, the larger-than-life and the obvious-to-the-edge-of-vulgarity are not only forgivable, they are often highly effective in characterization, situation and language.

But to leave the subject of medium at this point would be misleading. *Under Milk Wood* is not simply a play: it is a play *for Voices*. The medium is intermediate between a play and a poem, allowing and calling for characteristics shared by both. Embedded in the broadest passages, the roughest prose, the listener or the reader-listener will find some fine poetry, for example, in the Captain Cat-Rosie Probert dialogues – incidentally, Thomas's own favourite parts of the play. Captain Cat and the narrators serve as eyes only in a certain sense; the play, whether heard in the mind or from a stage, is meant for the ear, which, unlike the eye, imposes no limits upon the imagination.

The success of *Under Milk Wood* in translation is significant. Verbal subtlety, word-play, the rhythm and the essence of the poetry, the strongly individual style of the 'prose' – if that is what we can call it – all these are lost in the process of translation. What is left? Humour, characterization, images, structure, the forward movement of the play (the word 'plot' can hardly be used), and robustness. If I had to choose one word to describe the quality that has ensured the survival of the play after the ordeal of translation, I would choose 'vitality'.

In my Preface of twenty years ago there is one paragraph which I feel I should modify in the light of subsequent knowledge and reflection. In the first paragraph, leaning a little heavily on editorial privilege, I imply that *Under Milk Wood* was completed; at the same time I mention the lack of final revision and express an opinion I still hold: 'we are justified in regarding what [Thomas] has left as a complete work'. Here it could be argued that this is a quibble on the words 'completed' and 'complete'. For us, *Under Milk Wood* is complete; for Dylan Thomas it was not completed. Quite apart from the work of revision, he intended to add a great deal to the evening sequence which, as it stands, is disproportionately short. He showed me some of this material. What I saw consisted chiefly of fragments of ballads to be sung by some of the main characters, for example, Bessie Bighead; the evening, like the morning, was to be 'all singing'. Even from these fragments, it was possible to guess how the ballads would turn out: the style would be 'mock sentimental eighteenth century', with some sexual innuendoes thrown in – like Mr Waldo's song, in fact. Llareggub's evening was evidently planned to be a celebration of maudlin drunkenness and ribaldry, and the date of events, from the vague 'recent present' of the opening of the play, was to slip back still further into the eighteenth century, the century in which Polly Garter always had lived.

The incompleteness of *Under Milk Wood* caused textual difficulties, which were aggravated by Thomas's own alteration of words or phrases to suit American audiences. From a strictly scientific point of view only a variorum edition could unfold the whole story of deletions, substitutions, second thoughts, projected ideas, alternatives and so on. In my opinion, such an edition would be suitable only for the kind of reader who should never read *Under Milk Wood* at all; the play does not invite an academic approach. If this is true, textual responsibility in any edition of the play falls squarely on the shoulders of the editor, for good or for ill. My own aim has been to present a plain readable text, without fuss or distraction, and, above all, without additional reading or speaking directions, which serve only to limit the freedom of the reader's imagination. The text itself is already rich enough in suggestion and atmosphere.

Twenty years have taught me that something must also be said about the importance of the music in *Under Milk Wood*. To give one example: I have heard productions and public readings in which the Waldo Song was omitted. The disproportion of the evening sequence exists already; the omission of the song reduces that sequence to the proportion of a withered limb in the body of the play. Unfortunately, we are without the other ballads intended for the evening sequence, but at least we have the Waldo song. Another point I would like to make concerns the casting of Polly Garter and Waldo. Obviously, these two characters, one of whom has almost nothing to say, should not be tone-deaf. On the other hand, they should not be professional singers. There is no music in *Under Milk Wood* meant to be performed with accuracy and polish; it should be sung as it would have been sung in Llareggub. In the finest public reading of *Under Milk Wood* I have ever heard – it was presented by players with real (not assumed) *South*-Walian accents – Waldo gave a rough, inaccurate, free interpretation of his song, and the whole cast joined in the refrain wildly, with abandon. The aim of this passage in the play had been achieved: here was the real pub atmosphere, after too-much-to-drink, and the sense of a time passed in carousing and singing was satisfied.

One last word about a word. At the time of first publication I was obliged against my will to change the name Llareggub to Llaregyb. In this edition I am glad to have the opportunity to see that the correct spelling is restored.

August 1974   DANIEL JONES

Under Milk Wood

[*Silence*]

FIRST VOICE (*Very softly*)
To begin at the beginning:
It is spring, moonless night in the small town, starless
and bible-black, the cobblestreets silent and the
hunched, courters'-and-rabbits' wood limping
invisible down to the sloeblack, slow, black,
crowblack, fishingboat-bobbing sea. The houses are
blind as moles (though moles see fine to-night in the
snouting, velvet dingles) or blind as Captain Cat there
in the muffled middle by the pump and the town
clock, the shops in mourning, the Welfare Hall in
widows' weeds. And all the people of the lulled and
dumbfound town are sleeping now.

Hush, the babies are sleeping, the farmers, the
fishers, the tradesmen and pensioners, cobbler,
school-teacher, postman and publican, the undertaker
and the fancy woman, drunkard, dressmaker,
preacher, policeman, the webfoot cocklewomen and
the tidy wives. Young girls lie bedded soft or glide in
their dreams, with rings and trousseaux, bridesmaided
by glow-worms down the aisles of the organplaying
wood. The boys are dreaming wicked or of the
bucking ranches of the night and the jollyrodgered
sea. And the anthracite statues of the horses sleep in

the fields, and the cows in the byres, and the dogs in
the wetnosed yards; and the cats nap in the slant
corners or lope sly, streaking and needling, on the one
cloud of the roofs.

You can hear the dew falling, and the hushed town
breathing. Only *your* eyes are unclosed to see the
black and folded town fast, and slow, asleep. And you
alone can hear the invisible starfall, the darkest-
before-dawn minutely dewgrazed stir of the black,
dab-filled sea where the *Arethusa*, the *Curlew* and the
Skylark, Zanzibar, Rhiannon, the *Rover*, the
Cormorant, and the *Star of Wales* tilt and ride.

Listen. It is night moving in the streets, the
processional salt slow musical wind in Coronation
Street and Cockle Row, it is the grass growing on
Llareggub Hill, dewfall, starfall, the sleep of birds in
Milk Wood.

Listen. It is night in the chill, squat chapel, hymning
in bonnet and brooch and bombazine black, butterfly
choker and bootlace bow, coughing like nannygoats,
sucking mintoes, fortywinking hallelujah; night in the
four-ale, quiet as a domino; in Ocky Milkman's loft
like a mouse with gloves; in Dai Bread's bakery flying
like black flour. It is to-night in Donkey Street,
trotting silent, with seaweed on its hooves, along the
cockled cobbles, past curtained fernpot, text and
trinket, harmonium, holy dresser, watercolours done
by hand, china dog and rosy tin teacaddy. It is night
neddying among the snuggeries of babies.

Look. It is night, dumbly, royally winding through
the Coronation cherry trees; going through the
graveyard of Bethesda with winds gloved and folded,
and dew doffed; tumbling by the Sailors Arms.

Time passes. Listen. Time passes.

Come closer now.

Only you can hear the houses sleeping in the streets in the slow deep salt and silent black, bandaged night. Only you can see, in the blinded bedrooms, the coms. and petticoats over the chairs, the jugs and basins, the glasses of teeth, Thou Shalt Not on the wall, and the yellowing dickybird-watching pictures of the dead. Only you can hear and see, behind the eyes of the sleepers, the movements and countries and mazes and colours and dismays and rainbows and tunes and wishes and flight and fall and despairs and big seas of their dreams.

From where you are, you can hear their dreams.

Captain Cat, the retired blind sea-captain, asleep in his bunk in the seashelled, ship-in-bottled, shipshape best cabin of Schooner House dreams of

SECOND VOICE

never such seas as any that swamped the decks of his S.S. *Kidwelly* bellying over the bedclothes and jellyfish-slippery sucking him down salt deep into the Davy dark where the fish come biting out and nibble him down to his wishbone, and the long drowned nuzzle up to him.

FIRST DROWNED

Remember me, Captain?

CAPTAIN CAT

You're Dancing Williams!

FIRST DROWNED

I lost my step in Nantucket.

[3]

SECOND DROWNED
Do you see me, Captain? the white bone talking? I'm
Tom-Fred the donkeyman . . . we shared the same
girl once . . . her name was Mrs Probert . . .

WOMAN'S VOICE
Rosie Probert, thirty three Duck Lane. Come on up,
boys, I'm dead.

THIRD DROWNED
Hold me, Captain, I'm Jonah Jarvis, come to a bad
end, very enjoyable.

FOURTH DROWNED
Alfred Pomeroy Jones, sea-lawyer, born in Mumbles,
sung like a linnet, crowned you with a flagon, tattooed
with mermaids, thirst like a dredger, died of blisters.

FIRST DROWNED
This skull at your earhole is

FIFTH DROWNED
Curly Bevan. Tell my auntie it was me that pawned
the ormolu clock.

CAPTAIN CAT
Aye, aye, Curly.

SECOND DROWNED
Tell my missus no I never

THIRD DROWNED
I never done what she said I never.

FOURTH DROWNED
Yes they did.

FIFTH DROWNED
And who brings coconuts and shawls and parrots to
my Gwen now?

FIRST DROWNED
How's it above?

SECOND DROWNED
Is there rum and laverbread?

THIRD DROWNED
Bosoms and robins?

FOURTH DROWNED
Concertinas?

FIFTH DROWNED
Ebenezer's bell?

FIRST DROWNED
Fighting and onions?

SECOND DROWNED
And sparrows and daisies?

THIRD DROWNED
Tiddlers in a jamjar?

FOURTH DROWNED
Buttermilk and whippets?

[5]

FIFTH DROWNED
Rock-a-bye baby?

FIRST DROWNED
Washing on the line?

SECOND DROWNED
And old girls in the snug?

THIRD DROWNED
How's the tenors in Dowlais?

FOURTH DROWNED
Who milks the cows in Maesgwyn?

FIFTH DROWNED
When she smiles, is there dimples?

FIRST DROWNED
What's the smell of parsley?

CAPTAIN CAT
Oh, my dead dears!

FIRST VOICE
From where you are you can hear in Cockle Row in the spring, moonless night, Miss Price, dressmaker and sweetshop-keeper, dream of

SECOND VOICE
her lover, tall as the town clock tower, Samson-syrup-gold-maned, whacking thighed and piping hot, thunderbolt-bass'd and barnacle-breasted, flailing up the cockles with his eyes like blowlamps and scooping low over her lonely loving hotwaterbottled body.

MR EDWARDS
Myfanwy Price!

MISS PRICE
Mr Mog Edwards!

MR EDWARDS
I am a draper mad with love. I love you more than all
the flannelette and calico, candlewick, dimity, crash
and merino, tussore, cretonne, crepon, muslin, poplin,
ticking and twill in the whole Cloth Hall of the world.
I have come to take you away to my Emporium on the
hill, where the change hums on wires. Throw away
your little bedsocks and your Welsh wool knitted
jacket, I will warm the sheets like an electric toaster, I
will lie by your side like the Sunday roast.

MISS PRICE
I will knit you a wallet of forget-me-not blue, for the
money to be comfy. I will warm your heart by the fire
so that you can slip it in under your vest when the
shop is closed.

MR EDWARDS
Myfanwy, Myfanwy, before the mice gnaw at your
bottom drawer will you say

MISS PRICE
Yes, Mog, yes, Mog, yes, yes, yes.

MR EDWARDS
And all the bells of the tills of the town shall ring for
our wedding.
                              [*Noise of money-tills and chapel bells*

FIRST VOICE

Come now, drift up the dark, come up the drifting
sea-dark street now in the dark night seesawing like
the sea, to the bible-black airless attic over Jack Black
the cobbler's shop where alone and savagely Jack
Black sleeps in a nightshirt tied to his ankles with
elastic and dreams of

SECOND VOICE

chasing the naughty couples down the grassgreen
gooseberried double bed of the wood, flogging the
tosspots in the spit-and-sawdust, driving out the bare
bold girls from the sixpenny hops of his nightmares.

JACK BLACK (*Loudly*)

Ach y fi!
Ach y fi!

FIRST VOICE

Evans the Death, the undertaker,

SECOND VOICE

laughs high and aloud in his sleep and curls up his toes
as he sees, upon waking fifty years ago, snow lie deep
on the goosefield behind the sleeping house; and he
runs out into the field where his mother is making
welsh-cakes in the snow, and steals a fistful of
snowflakes and currants and climbs back to bed to eat
them cold and sweet under the warm, white clothes
while his mother dances in the snow kitchen crying
out for her lost currants.

FIRST VOICE

And in the little pink-eyed cottage next to the

undertaker's, lie, alone, the seventeen snoring gentle
stone of Mister Waldo, rabbitcatcher, barber,
herbalist, catdoctor, quack, his fat pink hands, palms
up, over the edge of the patchwork quilt, his black
boots neat and tidy in the washing-basin, his bowler
on a nail above the bed, a milk stout and a slice of cold
bread pudding under the pillow; and, dripping in the
dark, he dreams of

MOTHER
 This little piggy went to market
 This little piggy stayed at home
 This little piggy had roast beef
 This little piggy had none
 And this little piggy went

LITTLE BOY
 wee wee wee wee wee

MOTHER
 all the way home to

WIFE (*Screaming*)
 Waldo! Wal-do!

MR WALDO
 Yes, Blodwen love?

WIFE
 Oh, what'll the neighbours say, what'll the
 neighbours . . .

FIRST NEIGHBOUR
 Poor Mrs Waldo

SECOND NEIGHBOUR
    What she puts up with

FIRST NEIGHBOUR
    Never should of married

SECOND NEIGHBOUR
    If she didn't had to

FIRST NEIGHBOUR
    Same as her mother

SECOND NEIGHBOUR
    There's a husband for you

FIRST NEIGHBOUR
    Bad as his father

SECOND NEIGHBOUR
    And you know where he ended

FIRST NEIGHBOUR
    Up in the asylum

SECOND NEIGHBOUR
    Crying for his ma

FIRST NEIGHBOUR
    Every Saturday

SECOND NEIGHBOUR
    He hasn't got a leg

FIRST NEIGHBOUR
    And carrying on

[10]

SECOND NEIGHBOUR
  With that Mrs Beattie Morris

FIRST NEIGHBOUR
  Up in the quarry

SECOND NEIGHBOUR
  And seen her baby

FIRST NEIGHBOUR
  It's got his nose

SECOND NEIGHBOUR
  Oh it makes my heart bleed

FIRST NEIGHBOUR
  What he'll do for drink

SECOND NEIGHBOUR
  He sold the pianola

FIRST NEIGHBOUR
  And her sewing machine

SECOND NEIGHBOUR
  Falling in the gutter

FIRST NEIGHBOUR
  Talking to the lamp-post

SECOND NEIGHBOUR
  Using language

FIRST NEIGHBOUR
  Singing in the w

SECOND NEIGHBOUR
 Poor Mrs Waldo

WIFE (*Tearfully*)
 . . . Oh, Waldo, Waldo!

MR WALDO
 Hush, love, hush. I'm *widower* Waldo now.

MOTHER (*Screaming*)
 Waldo, Wal-do!

LITTLE BOY
 Yes, our mam?

MOTHER
 Oh, what'll the neighbours say, what'll the
 neighbours . . .

THIRD NEIGHBOUR
 Black as a chimbley

FOURTH NEIGHBOUR
 Ringing doorbells

THIRD NEIGHBOUR
 Breaking windows

FOURTH NEIGHBOUR
 Making mudpies

THIRD NEIGHBOUR
 Stealing currants

FOURTH NEIGHBOUR
Chalking words

THIRD NEIGHBOUR
Saw him in the bushes

FOURTH NEIGHBOUR
Playing mwchins

THIRD NEIGHBOUR
Send him to bed without any supper

FOURTH NEIGHBOUR
Give him sennapods and lock him in the dark

THIRD NEIGHBOUR
Off to the reformatory

FOURTH NEIGHBOUR
Off to the reformatory

TOGETHER
Learn him with a slipper on his b.t.m.

ANOTHER MOTHER (*Screaming*)
Waldo, Wal-do! what you doing with our Matti?

LITTLE BOY
Give us a kiss, Matti Richards.

LITTLE GIRL
Give us a penny then.

MR WALDO
I only got a halfpenny.

FIRST WOMAN
    Lips is a penny.

PREACHER
    Will you take this woman Matti Richards

SECOND WOMAN
    Dulcie Prothero

THIRD WOMAN
    Effie Bevan

FOURTH WOMAN
    Lil the Gluepot

FIFTH WOMAN
    Mrs Flusher

WIFE
    Blodwen Bowen

PREACHER
    To be your awful wedded wife

LITTLE BOY (*Screaming*)
    No, no, no!

FIRST VOICE
    Now, in her iceberg-white, holily laundered crinoline
    nightgown, under virtuous polar sheets, in her spruced
    and scoured dust-defying bedroom in trig and trim
    Bay View, a house for paying guests, at the top of the
    town, Mrs Ogmore-Pritchard widow, twice, of Mr
    Ogmore, linoleum, retired, and Mr Pritchard, failed

[14]

bookmaker, who maddened by besoming, swabbing and scrubbing, the voice of the vacuum-cleaner and the fume of polish, ironically swallowed disinfectant, fidgets in her rinsed sleep, wakes in a dream, and nudges in the ribs dead Mr Ogmore, dead Mr Pritchard, ghostly on either side.

MRS OGMORE-PRITCHARD
Mr Ogmore!
Mr Pritchard!
It is time to inhale your balsam.

MR OGMORE
Oh, Mrs Ogmore!

MR PRITCHARD
Oh, Mrs Pritchard!

MRS OGMORE-PRITCHARD
Soon it will be time to get up.
Tell me your tasks, in order.

MR OGMORE
I must put my pyjamas in the drawer marked pyjamas.

MR PRITCHARD
I must take my cold bath which is good for me.

MR OGMORE
I must wear my flannel band to ward off sciatica.

MR PRITCHARD
I must dress behind the curtain and put on my apron.

MR OGMORE
>I must blow my nose.

MRS OGMORE-PRITCHARD
>In the garden, if you please.

MR OGMORE
>In a piece of tissue-paper which I afterwards burn.

MR PRITCHARD
>I must take my salts which are nature's friend.

MR OGMORE
>I must boil the drinking water because of germs.

MR PRITCHARD
>I must make my herb tea which is free from tannin.

MR OGMORE
>And have a charcoal biscuit which is good for me.

MR PRITCHARD
>I may smoke one pipe of asthma mixture.

MRS OGMORE-PRITCHARD
>In the woodshed, if you please.

MR PRITCHARD
>And dust the parlour and spray the canary.

MR OGMORE
>I must put on rubber gloves and search the peke for fleas.

MR PRITCHARD

I must dust the blinds and then I must raise them.

MRS OGMORE-PRITCHARD

And before you let the sun in, mind it wipes its shoes.

FIRST VOICE

In Butcher Beynon's, Gossamer Beynon, daughter, schoolteacher, dreaming deep, daintily ferrets under a fluttering hummock of chicken's feathers in a slaughterhouse that has chintz curtains and a three-pieced suite, and finds, with no surprise, a small rough ready man with a bushy tail winking in a paper carrier.

GOSSAMER BEYNON

At last, my love,

FIRST VOICE

sighs Gossamer Beynon. And the bushy tail wags rude and ginger.

ORGAN MORGAN

Help,

SECOND VOICE

cries Organ Morgan, the organist, in his dream,

ORGAN MORGAN

There is perturbation and music in Coronation Street! All the spouses are honking like geese and the babies singing opera. P.C. Attila Rees has got his truncheon out and is playing cadenzas by the pump, the cows from Sunday Meadow ring like reindeer, and on the

roof of Handel Villa see the Women's Welfare
hoofing, bloomered, in the moon.

FIRST VOICE
At the sea-end of town, Mr and Mrs Floyd, the
cocklers, are sleeping as quiet as death, side by
wrinkled side, toothless, salt and brown, like two old
kippers in a box.
  And high above, in Salt Lake Farm, Mr Utah
Watkins counts, all night, the wife-faced sheep as they
leap the fences on the hill, smiling and knitting and
bleating just like Mrs Utah Watkins.

UTAH WATKINS (*Yawning*)
Thirty-four, thirty-five, thirty-six, forty-eight, eighty-
nine . . .

MRS UTAH WATKINS (*Bleating*)
Knit one slip one
Knit two together
Pass the slipstitch over . . .

FIRST VOICE
Ocky Milkman, drowned asleep in Cockle Street,
is emptying his churns into the Dewi River,

OCKY MILKMAN (*Whispering*)
regardless of expense,

FIRST VOICE
and weeping like a funeral.

SECOND VOICE
Cherry Owen, next door, lifts a tankard to his lips but

nothing flows out of it. He shakes the tankard. It
turns into a fish. He drinks the fish.

FIRST VOICE

P.C. Attila Rees lumps out of bed, dead to the dark
and still foghorning, and drags out his helmet from
under the bed; but deep in the backyard lock-up of
his sleep a mean voice murmurs.

A VOICE (*Murmuring*)

You'll be sorry for this in the morning,

FIRST VOICE

and he heave-ho's back to bed. His helmet swashes in
the dark.

SECOND VOICE

Willy Nilly, postman, asleep up street, walks fourteen
miles to deliver the post as he does every day of the
night, and rat-a-tats hard and sharp on Mrs Willy
Nilly.

MRS WILLY NILLY

Don't spank me, please, teacher,

SECOND VOICE

whimpers his wife at his side, but every night of her
married life she has been late for school.

FIRST VOICE

Sinbad Sailors, over the taproom of the Sailors Arms,
hugs his damp pillow whose secret name is Gossamer
Beynon.
     A mogul catches Lily Smalls in the wash-house.

LILY SMALLS

Ooh, you old mogul!

SECOND VOICE

Mrs Rose Cottage's eldest, Mae, peels off her pink-and-white skin in a furnace in a tower in a cave in a waterfall in a wood and waits there raw as an onion for Mister Right to leap up the burning tall hollow splashes of leaves like a brilliantined trout.

MAE ROSE COTTAGE (*Very close and softly, drawing out*
the words)

Call me Dolores
Like they do in the stories.

FIRST VOICE

Alone until she dies, Bessie Bighead, hired help, born in the workhouse, smelling of the cowshed, snores bass and gruff on a couch of straw in a loft in Salt Lake Farm and picks a posy of daisies in Sunday Meadow to put on the grave of Gomer Owen who kissed her once by the pig-sty when she wasn't looking and never kissed her again although she was looking all the time.

And the Inspectors of Cruelty fly down into Mrs Butcher Beynon's dream to persecute Mr Benyon for selling

BUTCHER BEYNON

owlmeat, dogs' eyes, manchop.

SECOND VOICE

Mr Beynon, in butcher's bloodied apron, spring-heels down Coronation Street, a finger, not his own, in his

[20]

mouth. Straightfaced in his cunning sleep he pulls the legs of his dreams and

BUTCHER BEYNON
hunting on pigback shoots down the wild giblets.

ORGAN MORGAN (*High and softly*)
Help!

GOSSAMER BEYNON (*Softly*)
My foxy darling.

FIRST VOICE
Now behind the eyes and secrets of the dreamers in the streets rocked to sleep by the sea, see the

SECOND VOICE
titbits and topsyturvies, bobs and buttontops, bags and bones, ash and rind and dandruff and nailparings, saliva and snowflakes and moulted feathers of dreams, the wrecks and sprats and shells and fishbones, whalejuice and moonshine and small salt fry dished up by the hidden sea.

FIRST VOICE
The owls are hunting. Look, over Bethesda gravestones one hoots and swoops and catches a mouse by Hannah Rees, Beloved Wife. And in Coronation Street, which you alone can see it is so dark under the chapel in the skies, the Reverend Eli Jenkins, poet, preacher, turns in his deep towards-dawn sleep and dreams of

REV. ELI JENKINS
Eisteddfodau.

SECOND VOICE

He intricately rhymes, to the music of crwth and pibgorn, all night long in his druid's seedy nightie in a beer-tent black with parchs.

FIRST VOICE

Mr Pugh, schoolmaster, fathoms asleep, pretends to be sleeping, spies foxy round the droop of his nightcap and psst! whistles up

MR PUGH

Murder.

FIRST VOICE

Mrs Organ Morgan, groceress, coiled grey like a dormouse, her paws to her ears, conjures

MRS ORGAN MORGAN

Silence.

SECOND VOICE

She sleeps very dulcet in a cove of wool, and trumpeting Organ Morgan at her side snores no louder than a spider.

FIRST VOICE

Mary Ann Sailors dreams of

MARY ANN SAILORS

The Garden of Eden.

FIRST VOICE

She comes in her smock-frock and clogs

MARY ANN SAILORS
  away from the cool scrubbed cobbled kitchen with the
  Sunday-school pictures on the whitewashed wall and
  the farmers' almanac hung above the settle and the
  sides of bacon on the ceiling hooks, and goes down the
  cockleshelled paths of that applepie kitchen garden,
  ducking under the gippo's clothespegs, catching her
  apron on the blackcurrant bushes, past beanrows and
  onion-bed and tomatoes ripening on the wall towards
  the old man playing the harmonium in the orchard,
  and sits down on the grass at his side and shells the
  green peas that grow up through the lap of her
  frock that brushes the dew.

FIRST VOICE
  In Donkey Street, so furred with sleep, Dai Bread,
  Polly Garter, Nogood Boyo, and Lord Cut-Glass
  sigh before the dawn that is about to be and dream of

DAI BREAD
  Harems.

POLLY GARTER
  Babies.

NOGOOD BOYO
  Nothing.

LORD CUT-GLASS
  Tick tock tick tock tick tock tick tock.

FIRST VOICE
  Time passes. Listen. Time passes. An owl flies home

past Bethesda, to a chapel in an oak. And the dawn
inches up.

> [*One distant bell-note, faintly reverberating*

Stand on this hill. This is Llareggub Hill, old as the
hills, high, cool, and green, and from this small circle
of stones, made not by druids but by Mrs Beynon's
Billy, you can see all the town below you sleeping in
the first of the dawn.

You can hear the love-sick woodpigeons mooning
in bed. A dog barks in his sleep, farmyards away. The
town ripples like a lake in the waking haze.

VOICE OF A GUIDE-BOOK
Less than five hundred souls inhabit the three quaint
streets and the few narrow by-lanes and scattered
farmsteads that constitute this small, decaying
watering-place which may, indeed, be called a
'backwater of life' without disrespect to its natives
who possess, to this day, a salty individuality of their
own. The main street, Coronation Street, consists, for
the most part, of humble, two-storied houses many of
which attempt to achieve some measure of gaiety by
prinking themselves out in crude colours and by the
liberal use of pinkwash, though there are remaining a
few eighteenth-century houses of more pretension, if,
on the whole, in a sad state of disrepair. Though there
is little to attract the hillclimber, the healthseeker, the
sportsman, or the weekending motorist, the
contemplative may, if sufficiently attracted to spare it
some leisurely hours, find, in its cobbled streets and its
little fishing harbour, in its several curious customs,

and in the conversation of its local 'characters', some of that picturesque sense of the past so frequently lacking in towns and villages which have kept more abreast of the times. The River Dewi is said to abound in trout, but is much poached. The one place of worship, with its neglected graveyard, is of no architectural interest.

[*A cock crows*

FIRST VOICE

The principality of the sky lightens now, over our green hill, into spring morning larked and crowed and belling.

[*Slow bell notes*

FIRST VOICE

Who pulls the townhall bellrope but blind Captain Cat? One by one, the sleepers are rung out of sleep this one morning as every morning. And soon you shall see the chimneys' slow upflying snow as Captain Cat, in sailor's cap and seaboots, announces to-day with his loud get-out-of-bed bell.

SECOND VOICE

The Reverend Eli Jenkins, in Bethesda House, gropes out of bed into his preacher's black, combs back his bard's white hair, forgets to wash, pads barefoot downstairs, opens the front door, stands in the doorway and, looking out at the day and up at the eternal hill, and hearing the sea break and the gab of birds, remembers his own verses and tells them softly to empty Coronation Street that is rising and raising its blinds.

[25]

Dear Gwalia! I know there are
Towns lovelier than ours,
And fairer hills and loftier far,
And groves more full of flowers,

And boskier woods more blithe with spring
And bright with birds' adorning,
And sweeter bards than I to sing
Their praise this beauteous morning.

By Cader Idris, tempest-torn,
Or Moel yr Wyddfa's glory,
Carnedd Llewelyn beauty born,
Plinlimmon old in story,

By mountains where King Arthur dreams,
By Penmaenmawr defiant,
Llareggub Hill a molehill seems,
A pygmy to a giant.

By Sawdde, Senny, Dovey, Dee,
Edw, Eden, Aled, all,
Taff and Towy broad and free,
Llyfnant with its waterfall,

Claerwen, Cleddau, Dulais, Daw,
Ely, Gwili, Ogwr, Nedd,
Small is our River Dewi, Lord,
A baby on a rushy bed.

By Carreg Cennen, King of time,
Our Heron Head is only
A bit of stone with seaweed spread
Where gulls come to be lonely.

A tiny dingle is Milk Wood
By Golden Grove 'neath Grongar,
But let me choose and oh! I should
Love all my life and longer

To stroll among our trees and stray
In Goosegog Lane, on Donkey Down,
And hear the Dewi sing all day,
And never, never leave the town.

SECOND VOICE

The Reverend Jenkins closes the front door. His
morning service is over.

[*Slow bell notes*

FIRST VOICE

Now, woken at last by the out-of-bed-sleepy-head-
Polly-put-the-kettle-on townhall bell, Lily Smalls,
Mrs Beynon's treasure, comes downstairs from a
dream of royalty who all night long went larking with
her full of sauce in the Milk Wood dark, and puts the
kettle on the primus ring in Mrs Beynon's kitchen,
and looks at herself in Mr Beynon's shaving-glass
over the sink, and sees:

LILY SMALLS

Oh there's a face!
Where you get that hair from?
Got it from a old tom cat.
Give it back then, love.
Oh there's a perm!

Where you get that nose from, Lily?
Got it from my father, silly.
You've got it on upside down!
Oh there's a conk!

Look at your complexion!
Oh no, *you* look.
Needs a bit of make-up.
Needs a veil.
Oh there's glamour!

Where you get that smile, Lil?
Never you mind, girl.
Nobody loves you.
That's what *you* think.

Who is it loves you?
Shan't tell.
Come on, Lily.
Cross your heart then?
Cross my heart.

FIRST VOICE
    And very softly, her lips almost touching her
    reflection, she breathes the name and clouds the
    shaving-glass.

MRS BEYNON (*Loudly, from above*)
    Lily!

LILY SMALLS (*Loudly*)
    Yes, mum.

MRS BEYNON
    Where's my tea, girl?

LILY SMALLS

(*Softly*) Where d'you think? In the cat-box?
(*Loudly*) Coming up, mum.

FIRST VOICE

Mr Pugh, in the School House opposite, takes up the
morning tea to Mrs Pugh, and whispers on the stairs

MR PUGH

Here's your arsenic, dear.
And your weedkiller biscuit.
I've throttled your parakeet.
I've spat in the vases.
I've put cheese in the mouseholes.
Here's your . . .
. . . nice tea, dear.

MRS PUGH

Too much sugar.

MR PUGH

You haven't tasted it yet, dear.

MRS PUGH

Too much milk, then. Has Mr Jenkins said his poetry?

MR PUGH

Yes, dear.

MRS PUGH

Then it's time to get up. Give me my glasses.
No, not my *reading* glasses, I want to look *out*. I want
to see.

SECOND VOICE
     Lily Smalls the treasure down on her red knees
     washing the front step.

MRS PUGH
     She's tucked her dress in her bloomers – oh, the
     baggage!

SECOND VOICE
     P.C. Attila Rees, ox-broad, barge-booted, stamping
     out of Handcuff House in a heavy beef-red huff,
     black-browed under his damp helmet . . .

MRS PUGH
     He's going to arrest Polly Garter, mark my words.

MR PUGH
     What for, dear?

MRS PUGH
     For having babies.

SECOND VOICE
     . . . and lumbering down towards the strand to see
     that the sea is still there.

FIRST VOICE
     Mary Ann Sailors, opening her bedroom window
     above the taproom and calling out to the heavens

MARY ANN SAILORS
     I'm eighty-five years three months and a day!

MR PUGH
     I will say this for her, she never makes a mistake.

FIRST VOICE
Organ Morgan at his bedroom window playing
chords on the sill to the morning fishwife gulls who,
heckling over Donkey Street, observe

DAI BREAD
Me, Dai Bread, hurrying to the bakery, pushing in my
shirt-tails, buttoning my waistcoat, ping goes a
button, why can't they sew them, no time for
breakfast, nothing for breakfast, there's wives for you.

MRS DAI BREAD ONE
Me, Mrs Dai Bread One, capped and shawled and no
old corset, nice to be comfy, nice to be nice, clogging
on the cobbles to stir up a neighbour. Oh, Mrs Sarah,
can you spare a loaf, love? Dai Bread forgot the bread.
There's a lovely morning! How's your boils this
morning? Isn't that good news now, it's a change to sit
down. Ta, Mrs Sarah.

MRS DAI BREAD TWO
Me, Mrs Dai Bread Two, gypsied to kill in a silky
scarlet petticoat above my knees, dirty pretty knees,
see my body through my petticoat brown as a berry,
high-heel shoes with one heel missing, tortoiseshell
comb in my bright black slinky hair, nothing else at all
but a dab of scent, lolling gaudy at the doorway, tell
your fortune in the tea-leaves, scowling at the
sunshine, lighting up my pipe.

LORD CUT-GLASS
Me, Lord Cut-Glass, in an old frock-coat belonged to
Eli Jenkins and a pair of postman's trousers from
Bethesda Jumble, running out of doors to empty slops
– mind there, Rover! – and then running in again, tick
tock.

[31]

NOGOOD BOYO

Me, Nogood Boyo, up to no good in the wash-house.

MISS PRICE

Me, Miss Price, in my pretty print housecoat, deft at the clothesline, natty as a jenny-wren, then pit-pat back to my egg in its cosy, my crisp toast-fingers, my home-made plum and butterpat.

POLLY GARTER

Me, Polly Garter, under the washing line, giving the breast in the garden to my bonny new baby. Nothing grows in our garden, only washing. And babies. And where's their fathers live, my love? Over the hills and far away. You're looking up at me now. I know what you're thinking, you poor little milky creature. You're thinking, you're no better than you should be, Polly, and that's good enough for me. Oh, isn't life a terrible thing, thank God?

[*Single long high chord on strings*

FIRST VOICE

Now frying-pans spit, kettles and cats purr in the kitchen. The town smells of seaweed and breakfast all the way down from Bay View, where Mrs Ogmore-Pritchard, in smock and turban, big-besomed to engage the dust, picks at her starchless bread and sips lemon-rind tea, to Bottom Cottage, where Mr Waldo, in bowler and bib, gobbles his bubble-and-squeak and kippers and swigs from the saucebottle. Mary Ann Sailors

MARY ANN SAILORS

praises the Lord who made porridge.

[32]

FIRST VOICE
Mr Pugh

MR PUGH
remembers ground glass as he juggles his omelet.

FIRST VOICE
Mrs Pugh

MRS PUGH
nags the salt-cellar.

FIRST VOICE
Willy Nilly postman

WILLY NILLY
downs his last bucket of black brackish tea and
rumbles out bandy to the clucking back where the
hens twitch and grieve for their tea-soaked sops.

FIRST VOICE
Mrs Willy Nilly

MRS WILLY NILLY
full of tea to her double-chinned brim broods and
bubbles over her coven of kettles on the hissing hot
range always ready to steam open the mail.

FIRST VOICE
The Reverend Eli Jenkins

REV. ELI JENKINS
finds a rhyme and dips his pen in his cocoa.

FIRST VOICE

Lord Cut-Glass in his ticking kitchen

LORD CUT-GLASS

scampers from clock to clock, a bunch of clock-keys in
one hand, a fish-head in the other.

FIRST VOICE

Captain Cat in his galley

CAPTAIN CAT

blind and fine-fingered savours his sea-fry.

FIRST VOICE

Mr and Mrs Cherry Owen, in their Donkey Street
room that is bedroom, parlour, kitchen, and scullery,
sit down to last night's supper of onions boiled in
their overcoats and broth of spuds and baconrind and
leeks and bones.

MRS CHERRY OWEN

See that smudge on the wall by the picture of Auntie
Blossom? That's where you threw the sago.
                              [*Cherry Owen laughs with delight*

MRS CHERRY OWEN

You only missed me by an inch.

CHERRY OWEN

I always miss Auntie Blossom too.

[34]

MRS CHERRY OWEN

Remember last night? In you reeled, my boy, as
drunk as a deacon with a big wet bucket and a fish-
frail full of stout and you looked at me and you said,
'God has come home!' you said, and then over the
bucket you went, sprawling and bawling, and the
floor was all flagons and eels.

CHERRY OWEN

Was I wounded?

MRS CHERRY OWEN

And then you took off your trousers and you said,
'Does anybody want a fight!' Oh, you old baboon.

CHERRY OWEN

Give me a kiss.

MRS CHERRY OWEN

And then you sang 'Bread of Heaven', tenor and bass.

CHERRY OWEN

I *always* sing 'Bread of Heaven'.

MRS CHERRY OWEN

And then you did a little dance on the table.

CHERRY OWEN

I did?

MRS CHERRY OWEN

Drop dead!

CHERRY OWEN
    And then what did I do?

MRS CHERRY OWEN
    Then you cried like a baby and said you were a poor
    drunk orphan with nowhere to go but the grave.

CHERRY OWEN
    And what did I do next, my dear?

MRS CHERRY OWEN
    Then you danced on the table all over again and
    said you were King Solomon Owen and I was your
    Mrs Sheba.

CHERRY OWEN (*Softly*)
    And then?

MRS CHERRY OWEN
    And then I got you into bed and you snored all night
    like a brewery.
    [*Mr and Mrs Cherry Owen laugh delightedly together*

FIRST VOICE
    From Beynon Butchers in Coronation Street, the smell
    of fried liver sidles out with onions on its breath. And
    listen! In the dark breakfast-room behind the shop,
    Mr and Mrs Beynon, waited upon by their treasure,
    enjoy, between bites, their everymorning hullabaloo,
    and Mrs Beynon slips the gristly bits under the
    tasselled tablecloth to her fat cat.
                                                    [*Cat purrs*

MRS BEYNON
  She likes the liver, Ben.

MR BEYNON
  She ought to do, Bess. It's her brother's.

MRS BEYNON (*Screaming*)
  Oh, d'you hear that, Lily?

LILY SMALLS
  Yes, mum.

MRS BEYNON
  We're eating pusscat.

LILY SMALLS
  Yes, mum.

MRS BEYNON
  Oh, you cat-butcher!

MR BEYNON
  It was doctored, mind.

MRS BEYNON (*Hysterical*)
  What's that got to do with it?

MR BEYNON
  Yesterday we had mole.

MRS BEYNON
  Oh, Lily, Lily!

MR BEYNON

Monday, otter. Tuesday, shrews.

[*Mrs Beynon screams*

LILY SMALLS

Go on, Mrs Beynon. He's the biggest liar in town.

MRS BEYNON

Don't you dare say that about Mr Beynon.

LILY SMALLS

Everybody knows it, mum.

MRS BEYNON

Mr Beynon never tells a lie. Do you, Ben?

MR BEYNON

No, Bess. And now I am going out after the corgies,
with my little cleaver.

MRS BEYNON

Oh, Lily, Lily!

FIRST VOICE

Up the street, in the Sailors Arms, Sinbad Sailors,
grandson of Mary Ann Sailors, draws a pint in the
sunlit bar. The ship's clock in the bar says half past
eleven. Half past eleven is opening time. The hands of
the clock have stayed still at half past eleven for fifty
years. It is always opening time in the Sailors Arms.

SINBAD

Here's to me, Sinbad.

[38]

FIRST VOICE

All over the town, babies and old men are cleaned
and put into their broken prams and wheeled on to
the sunlit cockled cobbles or out into the backyards
under the dancing underclothes, and left. A baby cries.

OLD MAN

I want my pipe and he wants his bottle.

[*School bell rings*

FIRST VOICE

Noses are wiped, heads picked, hair combed, paws
scrubbed, ears boxed, and the children shrilled off to
school.

SECOND VOICE

Fishermen grumble to their nets. Nogood Boyo goes
out in the dinghy *Zanzibar,* ships the oars, drifts
slowly in the dab-filled bay, and, lying on his back in
the unbaled water, among crabs' legs and tangled
lines, looks up at the spring sky.

NOGOOD BOYO (*Softly, lazily*)

I don't know who's up there and I don't care.

FIRST VOICE

He turns his head and looks up at Llareggub Hill,
and sees, among green lathered trees, the white houses
of the strewn away farms, where farmboys whistle,
dogs shout, cows low, but all too far away for him,
or you, to hear. And in the town, the shops squeak
open. Mr Edwards, in butterfly-collar and straw-hat
at the doorway of Manchester House, measures with
his eye the dawdlers-by for striped flannel shirts and

shrouds and flowery blouses, and bellows to himself
in the darkness behind his eye

MR EDWARDS (*Whispers*)
I love Miss Price.

FIRST VOICE
Syrup is sold in the post-office. A car drives to market,
full of fowls and a farmer. Milk-churns stand at
Coronation Corner like short silver policemen. And,
sitting at the open window of Schooner House, blind
Captain Cat hears all the morning of the town.
[*School bell in background. Children's voices.
The noise of children's feet on the cobbles*

CAPTAIN CAT (*Softly, to himself*)
Maggie Richards, Ricky Rhys, Tommy Powell, our
Sal, little Gerwain, Billy Swansea with the dog's voice,
one of Mr Waldo's, nasty Humphrey, Jackie with the
sniff . . . Where's Dicky's Albie? and the boys from
Ty-pant? Perhaps they got the rash again.
[*A sudden cry among the children's voices*

CAPTAIN CAT
Somebody's hit Maggie Richards. Two to one it's
Billy Swansea. Never trust a boy who barks.
[*A burst of yelping crying*
Right again! That's Billy.

FIRST VOICE
And the children's voices cry away.
[*Postman's rat-a-tat on door, distant*

[40]

CAPTAIN CAT (*Softly, to himself*)
That's Willy Nilly knocking at Bay View. Rat-a-tat,
very soft. The knocker's got a kid glove on. Who's
sent a letter to Mrs Ogmore-Pritchard?

[*Rat-a-tat, distant again*

CAPTAIN CAT
Careful now, she swabs the front glassy. Every step's
like a bar of soap. Mind your size twelveses. That old
Bessie would beeswax the lawn to make the birds slip.

WILLY NILLY
Morning, Mrs Ogmore-Pritchard.

MRS OGMORE-PRITCHARD
Good morning, postman.

WILLY NILLY
Here's a letter for you with stamped and addressed
envelope enclosed, all the way from Builth Wells. A
gentleman wants to study birds and can he have
accommodation for two weeks and a bath vegetarian.

MRS OGMORE-PRITCHARD
No.

WILLY NILLY (*Persuasively*)
You wouldn't know he was in the house, Mrs
Ogmore-Pritchard. He'd be out in the mornings at
the bang of dawn with his bag of breadcrumbs and his
little telescope . . .

MRS OGMORE-PRITCHARD

> And come home at all hours covered with feathers.
> I don't want persons in my nice clean rooms breathing
> all over the chairs . . .

WILLY NILLY

> Cross my heart, he won't breathe.

MRS OGMORE-PRITCHARD

> . . . and putting their feet on my carpets and sneezing
> on my china and sleeping in my sheets . . .

WILLY NILLY

> He only wants a *single* bed, Mrs Ogmore-Pritchard.
>
> > [*Door slams*

CAPTAIN CAT (*Softly*)

> And back she goes to the kitchen to polish the
> potatoes.

FIRST VOICE

> Captain Cat hears Willy Nilly's feet heavy on the
> distant cobbles.

CAPTAIN CAT

> One, two, three, four, five . . . That's Mrs Rose
> Cottage. What's to-day? To-day she gets the letter
> from her sister in Gorslas. How's the twin's teeth?
> He's stopping at School House.

WILLY NILLY

> Morning, Mrs Pugh. Mrs Ogmore-Pritchard won't
> have a gentleman in from Builth Wells because he'll
> sleep in her sheets, Mrs Rose Cottage's sister in
> Gorslas's twins have got to have them out . . .

MRS PUGH
    Give me the parcel.

WILLY NILLY
    It's for *Mr* Pugh, Mrs Pugh.

MRS PUGH
    Never you mind. What's inside it?

WILLY NILLY
    A book called *Lives of the Great Poisoners*.

CAPTAIN CAT
    That's Manchester House.

WILLY NILLY
    Morning, Mr Edwards. Very small news. Mrs
    Ogmore-Pritchard won't have birds in the house, and
    Mr Pugh's bought a book now on how to do in Mrs
    Pugh.

MR EDWARDS
    Have you got a letter from *her*?

WILLY NILLY
    Miss Price loves you with all her heart. Smelling of
    lavender to-day. She's down to the last of the elder-
    flower wine but the quince jam's bearing up and she's
    knitting roses on the doilies. Last week she sold three
    jars of boiled sweets, pound of humbugs, half a box
    of jellybabies and six coloured photos of Llareggub.
    Yours for ever. Then twenty-one X's.

MR EDWARDS

Oh, Willy Nilly, she's a ruby! Here's my letter. Put it into her hands now.

[*Slow feet on cobbles, quicker feet approaching*

CAPTAIN CAT

Mr Waldo hurrying to the Sailors Arms. Pint of stout with a egg in it. [*Footsteps stop*

(*Softly*) There's a letter for him.

WILLY NILLY

It's another paternity summons, Mr Waldo.

FIRST VOICE

The quick footsteps hurry on along the cobbles and up three steps to the Sailors Arms.

MR WALDO (*Calling out*)

Quick, Sinbad. Pint of stout. And no egg in.

FIRST VOICE

People are moving now up and down the cobbled street.

CAPTAIN CAT

All the women are out this morning, in the sun. You can tell it's Spring. There goes Mrs Cherry, you can tell her by her trotters, off she trots new as a daisy. Who's that talking by the pump? Mrs Floyd and Boyo, talking flatfish. What can you talk about flatfish? That's Mrs Dai Bread One, waltzing up the street like a jelly, every time she shakes it's slap slap slap. Who's that? Mrs Butcher Beynon with her pet black cat, it follows her everywhere, miaow and all. There goes

Mrs Twenty-Three, important, the sun gets up and goes down in her dewlap, when she shuts her eyes, it's night. High heels now, in the morning too, Mrs Rose Cottage's eldest Mae, seventeen and never been kissed ho ho, going young and milking under my window to the field with the nannygoats, she reminds me all the way. Can't hear what the women are gabbing round the pump. Same as ever. Who's having a baby, who blacked whose eye, seen Polly Garter giving her belly an airing, there should be a law, seen Mrs Beynon's new mauve jumper, it's her old grey jumper dyed, who's dead, who's dying, there's a lovely day, oh the cost of soapflakes!

[*Organ music, distant*

CAPTAIN CAT
Organ Morgan's at it early. You can tell it's Spring.

FIRST VOICE
And he hears the noise of milk-cans.

CAPTAIN CAT
Ocky Milkman on his round. I will say this, his milk's as fresh as the dew. Half dew it is. Snuffle on, Ocky, watering the town . . . Somebody's coming. Now the voices round the pump can see somebody coming. Hush, there's a hush! You can tell by the noise of the hush, it's Polly Garter. (*Louder*) Hullo, Polly, who's there?

POLLY GARTER (*Off*)
Me, love.

[45]

CAPTAIN CAT

That's Polly Garter. (*Softly*) Hullo, Polly my love, can you hear the dumb goose-hiss of the wives as they huddle and peck or flounce at a waddle away? Who cuddled you when? Which of their gandering hubbies moaned in Milk Wood for your naughty mothering arms and body like a wardrobe, love? Scrub the floors of the Welfare Hall for the Mothers' Union Social Dance, you're one mother won't wriggle her roly poly bum or pat her fat little buttery feet in that wedding-ringed holy to-night though the waltzing breadwinners snatched from the cosy smoke of the Sailors Arms will grizzle and mope.

[*A cock crows*

CAPTAIN CAT

Too late, cock, too late

SECOND VOICE

for the town's half over with its morning. The morning's busy as bees.

[*Organ music fades into silence*

FIRST VOICE

There's the clip clop of horses on the sunhoneyed cobbles of the humming streets, hammering of horse-shoes, gobble quack and cackle, tomtit twitter from the bird-ounced boughs, braying on Donkey Down. Bread is baking, pigs are grunting, chop goes the butcher, milk-churns bell, tills ring, sheep cough, dogs shout, saws sing. Oh, the Spring whinny and morning moo from the clog dancing farms, the gulls' gab and rabble on the boat-bobbing river and sea and the cockles bubbling in the sand, scamper of sanderlings,

[46]

curlew cry, crow caw, pigeon coo, clock strike, bull
bellow, and the ragged gabble of the beargarden
school as the women scratch and babble in Mrs Organ
Morgan's general shop where everything is sold:
custard, buckets, henna, rat-traps, shrimp-nets, sugar,
stamps, confetti, paraffin, hatchets, whistles.

FIRST WOMAN
Mrs Ogmore-Pritchard

SECOND WOMAN
la di da

FIRST WOMAN
got a man in Builth Wells

THIRD WOMAN
and he got a little telescope to look at birds

SECOND WOMAN
Willy Nilly said

THIRD WOMAN
Remember her first husband? He didn't need a
telescope

FIRST WOMAN
he looked at them undressing through the keyhole

THIRD WOMAN
and he used to shout Tallyho

SECOND WOMAN
but Mr Ogmore was a proper gentleman

FIRST WOMAN
    even though he hanged his collie.

THIRD WOMAN
    Seen Mrs Butcher Beynon?

SECOND WOMAN
    she said Butcher Beynon put dogs in the mincer

FIRST WOMAN
    go on, he's pulling her leg

THIRD WOMAN
    now don't you dare tell her that, there's a dear

SECOND WOMAN
    or she'll think he's trying to pull it off and eat it.

FOURTH WOMAN
    There's a nasty lot live here when you come to think.

FIRST WOMAN
    Look at that Nogood Boyo now

SECOND WOMAN
    too lazy to wipe his snout

THIRD WOMAN
    and going out fishing every day and all he ever
    brought back was a Mrs Samuels

FIRST WOMAN
    been in the water a week.

[48]

SECOND WOMAN
And look at Ocky Milkman's wife that nobody's ever seen

FIRST WOMAN
he keeps her in the cupboard with the empties

THIRD WOMAN
and think of Dai Bread with two wives

SECOND WOMAN
one for the daytime one for the night.

FOURTH WOMAN
Men are brutes on the quiet.

THIRD WOMAN
And how's Organ Morgan, Mrs Morgan?

FIRST WOMAN
you look dead beat

SECOND WOMAN
it's organ organ all the time with him

THIRD WOMAN
up every night until midnight playing the organ.

MRS ORGAN MORGAN
Oh, I'm a martyr to music.

FIRST VOICE
Outside, the sun springs down on the rough and tumbling town. It runs through the hedges of

Goosegog Lane, cuffing the birds to sing. Spring whips green down Cockle Row, and the shells ring out. Llareggub this snip of a morning is wildfruit and warm, the streets, fields, sands and waters springing in the young sun.

SECOND VOICE
Evans the Death presses hard with black gloves on the coffin of his breast in case his heart jumps out.

EVANS THE DEATH (*Harshly*)
Where's your dignity. Lie down.

SECOND VOICE
Spring stirs Gossamer Beynon schoolmistress like a spoon.

GOSSAMER BEYNON (*Tearfully*)
Oh, what can I do? I'll *never* be refined if I twitch.

SECOND VOICE
Spring this strong morning foams in a flame in Jack Black as he cobbles a high-heeled shoe for Mrs Dai Bread Two the gypsy, but he hammers it sternly out.

JACK BLACK (*To a hammer rhythm*)
There is *no leg* belonging to the foot that belongs to this shoe.

SECOND VOICE
The sun and the green breeze ship Captain Cat's sea-memory again.

[50]

CAPTAIN CAT

No, *I'll* take the mulatto, by God, who's captain here?
Parlez-vous jig jig, Madam?

SECOND VOICE

Mary Ann Sailors says very softly to herself as she
looks out at Llareggub Hill from the bedroom where
she was born

MARY ANN SAILORS (*Loudly*)

It is Spring in Llareggub in the sun in my old age,
and this is the Chosen Land.
[*A choir of children's voices suddenly cries out on
one, high, glad, long, sighing note*

FIRST VOICE

And in Willy Nilly the Postman's dark and sizzling
damp tea-coated misty pygmy kitchen where the
spittingcat kettles throb and hop on the range, Mrs
Willy Nilly steams open Mr Mog Edwards' letter to
Miss Myfanwy Price and reads it aloud to Willy
Nilly by the squint of the Spring sun through the one
sealed window running with tears, while the drugged,
bedraggled hens at the back door whimper and snivel
for the lickerish bog-black tea.

MRS WILLY NILLY

From Manchester House, Llareggub. Sole Prop: Mr
Mog Edwards (late of Twll), Linendraper, Haber-
dasher, Master Tailor, Costumier. For West End
Negligee, Lingerie, Teagowns, Evening Dress,
Trousseaux, Layettes. Also Ready to Wear for All
Occasions. Economical Outfitting for Agricultural
Employment Our Speciality, Wardrobes Bought.

Among Our Satisfied Customers Ministers of Religion
and J.P.'s. Fittings by Appointment. Advertising
Weekly in the *Twll Bugle*. Beloved Myfanwy Price
my Bride in Heaven,

MOG EDWARDS

I love you until Death do us part and then we shall be
together for ever and ever. A new parcel of ribbons
has come from Carmarthen to-day, all the colours in
the rainbow. I wish I could tie a ribbon in your hair a
white one but it cannot be. I dreamed last night you
were all dripping wet and you sat on my lap as the
Reverend Jenkins went down the street. I see you got a
mermaid in your lap he said and he lifted his hat. He is
a proper Christian. Not like Cherry Owen who said
you should have thrown her back he said. Business is
very poorly. Polly Garter bought two garters with
roses but she never got stockings so what is the use I
say. Mr Waldo tried to sell me a woman's nightie
outsize he said he found it and we know where. I sold
a packet of pins to Tom the Sailors to pick his teeth. If
this goes on I shall be in the workhouse. My heart is in
your bosom and yours is in mine. God be with you
always Myfanwy Price and keep you lovely for me in
His Heavenly Mansion. I must stop now and remain,
Your Eternal, Mog Edwards.

MRS WILLY NILLY

And then a little message with a rubber stamp. Shop
at Mog's!!!

FIRST VOICE

And Willy Nilly, rumbling, jockeys out again to the

three-seated shack called the House of Commons in the back where the hens weep, and sees, in sudden Springshine,

SECOND VOICE

herring gulls heckling down to the harbour where the fishermen spit and prop the morning up and eye the fishy sea smooth to the sea's end as it lulls in blue. Green and gold money, tobacco, tinned salmon, hats with feathers, pots of fish-paste, warmth for the winter-to-be, weave and leap in it rich and slippery in the flash and shapes of fishes through the cold sea-streets. But with blue lazy eyes the fishermen gaze at that milk-mild whispering water with no ruck or ripple as though it blew great guns and serpents and typhooned the town.

FISHERMAN

Too rough for fishing to-day.

SECOND VOICE

And they thank God, and gob at a gull for luck, and moss-slow and silent make their way uphill, from the still still sea, towards the Sailors Arms as the children
                                                    [School bell

FIRST VOICE

spank and scamper rough and singing out of school into the draggletail yard. And Captain Cat at his window says soft to himself the words of their song.

[53]

CAPTAIN CAT (*To the beat of the singing*)
>   Johnnie Crack and Flossie Snail
>   Kept their baby in a milking pail
>   Flossie Snail and Johnnie Crack
>   One would pull it out and one would put it back
>   O it's my turn now said Flossie Snail
>   To take the baby from the milking pail
>   And it's my turn now said Johnny Crack
>   To smack it on the head and put it back
>
>   Johnnie Crack and Flossie Snail
>   Kept their baby in a milking pail
>   One would put it back and one would pull it out
>   And all it had to drink was ale and stout
>   For Johnnie Crack and Flossie Snail
>   Always used to say that stout and ale
>   Was *good* for a baby in a milking pail.   [*Lond pause*

FIRST VOICE
>   The music of the spheres is heard distinctly over Milk
>   Wood. It is 'The Rustle of Spring'.

SECOND VOICE
>   A glee-party sings in Bethesda Graveyard, gay but
>   muffled.

FIRST VOICE
>   Vegetables make love above the tenors

SECOND VOICE
>   and dogs bark blue in the face.

FIRST VOICE
>   Mrs Ogmore-Pritchard belches in a teeny hanky and

chases the sunlight with a flywhisk, but even she cannot drive out the Spring: from one of the fingerbowls a primrose grows.

SECOND VOICE
Mrs Dai Bread One and Mrs Dai Bread Two are sitting outside their house in Donkey Lane, one darkly one plumply blooming in the quick, dewy sun. Mrs Dai Bread Two is looking into a crystal ball which she holds in the lap of her dirty yellow petticoat, hard against her hard dark thighs.

MRS DAI BREAD TWO
Cross my palm with silver. Out of our housekeeping money. Aah!

MRS DAI BREAD ONE
What d'you see, lovie?

MRS DAI BREAD TWO
I see a featherbed. With three pillows on it. And a text above the bed. I can't read what it says, there's great clouds blowing. Now they have blown away. God is Love, the text says.

MRS DAI BREAD ONE (*Delighted*)
That's *our* bed.

MRS DAI BREAD TWO
And now it's vanished. The sun's spinning like a top. Who's this coming out of the sun? It's a hairy little man with big pink lips. He got a wall eye.

MRS DAI BREAD ONE
It's Dai, it's Dai Bread!

MRS DAI BREAD TWO
    Ssh! The featherbed's floating back. The little man's
    taking his boots off. He's pulling his shirt over his
    head. He's beating his chest with his fists. He's
    climbing into bed.

MRS DAI BREAD ONE
    Go on, go on.

MRS DAI BREAD TWO
    There's *two* women in bed. He looks at them both,
    with his head cocked on one side. He's whistling
    through his teeth. Now he grips his little arms round
    one of the women.

MRS DAI BREAD ONE
    Which one, which one?

MRS DAI BREAD TWO
    I can't see any more. There's great clouds blowing
    again.

MRS DAI BREAD ONE
    Ach, the mean old clouds!
                    [*Pause. The children's singing fades*

FIRST VOICE
    The morning is all singing. The Reverend Eli Jenkins,
    busy on his morning calls, stops outside the Welfare
    Hall to hear Polly Garter as she scrubs the floors for
    the Mothers' Union Dance to-night.

POLLY GARTER (*Singing*)
>   I loved a man whose name was Tom
>   He was strong as a bear and two yards long
>   I loved a man whose name was Dick
>   He was big as a barrel and three feet thick
>   And I loved a man whose name was Harry
>   Six feet tall and sweet as a cherry
>   But the one I loved best awake or asleep
>   Was little Willy Wee and he's six feet deep.
>
>   O Tom Dick and Harry were three fine men
>   And I'll never have such loving again
>   But little Willy Wee who took me on his knee
>   Little Willy Wee was the man for me.
>
>   Now men from every parish round
>   Run after me and roll me on the ground
>   But whenever I love another man back
>   Johnnie from the Hill or Sailing Jack
>   I always think as they do what they please
>   Of Tom Dick and Harry who were tall as trees
>   And most I think when I'm by their side
>   Of little Willy Wee who downed and died.
>
>   O Tom Dick and Harry were three fine men
>   And I'll never have such loving again
>   But little Willy Wee who took me on his knee
>   Little Willy Weazel was the man for me.

REV. ELI JENKINS
>   Praise the Lord! We are a musical nation.

SECOND VOICE
>   And the Reverend Jenkins hurries on through the
>   town to visit the sick with jelly and poems.

[57]

FIRST VOICE

The town's as full as a lovebird's egg.

MR WALDO

There goes the Reverend,

FIRST VOICE

says Mr Waldo at the smoked herring brown window
of the unwashed Sailors Arms,

MR WALDO

with his brolly and his odes. Fill 'em up, Sinbad, I'm
on the treacle to-day.

SECOND VOICE

The silent fishermen flush down their pints.

SINBAD

Oh, Mr Waldo,

FIRST VOICE

sighs Sinbad Sailors,

SINBAD

I dote on that Gossamer Beynon. She's a lady all over.

FIRST VOICE

And Mr Waldo, who is thinking of a woman soft
as Eve and sharp as sciatica to share his bread-
pudding bed, answers

MR WALDO

No lady that I know is.

SINBAD

And if only grandma'd die, cross my heart I'd go down on my knees Mr Waldo and I'd say Miss Gossamer I'd say

CHILDREN'S VOICES

When birds do sing hey ding a ding a ding Sweet lovers love the Spring . . .

SECOND VOICE

Polly Garter sings, still on her knees,

POLLY GARTER

Tom Dick and Harry were three fine men And I'll never have such

CHILDREN

ding a ding

POLLY GARTER

again.

FIRST VOICE

And the morning school is over, and Captain Cat at his curtained schooner's porthole open to the Spring sun tides hears the naughty forfeiting children tumble and rhyme on the cobbles.

GIRLS' VOICES

Gwennie call the boys They make such a noise.

GIRL

Boys boys boys Come along to me.

[59]

GIRLS' VOICES
> Boys boys boys
> Kiss Gwennie where she says
> Or give her a penny.
> Go on, Gwennie.

GIRL
> Kiss me in Goosegog Lane
> Or give me a penny.
> What's your name?

FIRST BOY
> Billy.

GIRL
> Kiss me in Goosegog Lane Billy
> Or give me a penny silly.

FIRST BOY
> Gwennie Gwennie
> I kiss you in Goosegog Lane.
> Now I haven't got to give you a penny.

GIRLS' VOICES
> Boys boys boys
> Kiss Gwennie where she says
> Or give her a penny.
> Go on, Gwennie.

GIRL
> Kiss me on Llareggub Hill
> Or give me a penny.
> What's your name?

SECOND BOY

    Johnnie Cristo.

GIRL

    Kiss me on Llareggub Hill Johnnie Cristo
    Or give me a penny mister.

SECOND BOY

    Gwennie Gwennie
    I kiss you on Llareggub Hill.
    Now I haven't got to give you a penny.

GIRLS' VOICES

    Boys boys boys
    Kiss Gwennie where she says
    Or give her a penny.
    Go on, Gwennie.

GIRL

    Kiss me in Milk Wood
    Or give me a penny.
    What's your name?

THIRD BOY

    Dicky.

GIRL

    Kiss me in Milk Wood Dicky
    Or give me a penny quickly.

THIRD BOY

    Gwennie Gwennie
    I can't kiss you in Milk Wood.

GIRLS' VOICES
    Gwennie ask him why.

GIRL
    Why?

THIRD BOY
    Because my mother says I mustn't.

GIRLS' VOICES
    Cowardy cowardy custard
    Give Gwennie a penny.

GIRL
    Give me a penny.

THIRD BOY
    I haven't got any.

GIRLS' VOICES
    Put him in the river
    Up to his liver
    Quick quick Dirty Dick
    Beat him on the bum
    With a rhubarb stick.
    Aiee!
    Hush!

FIRST VOICE
    And the shrill girls giggle and master around him and
    squeal as they clutch and thrash, and he blubbers
    away downhill with his patched pants falling, and his
    tear-splashed blush burns all the way as the
    triumphant bird-like sisters scream with buttons in

their claws and the bully brothers hoot after him his
little nickname and his mother's shame and his
father's wickedness with the loose wild barefoot
women of the hovels of the hills. It all means nothing
at all, and, howling for his milky mum, for her cawl
and buttermilk and cowbreath and welshcakes and
the fat birth-smelling bed and moonlit kitchen of her
arms, he'll never forget as he paddles blind home
through the weeping end of the world. Then his
tormentors tussle and run to the Cockle Street
sweet-shop, their pennies sticky as honey, to buy from
Miss Myfanwy Price, who is cocky and neat as a
puff-bosomed robin and her small round buttocks
tight as ticks, gobstoppers big as wens that rainbow as
you suck, brandyballs, winegums, hundreds and
thousands, liquorice sweet as sick, nougat to tug and
ribbon out like another red rubbery tongue, gum to
glue in girls' curls, crimson cough-drops to spit blood,
ice-cream cornets, dandelion-and-burdock, raspberry
and cherryade, pop goes the weasel and the wind.

SECOND VOICE
Gossamer Beynon high-heels out of school. The sun
hums down through the cotton flowers of her dress
into the bell of her heart and buzzes in the honey there
and couches and kisses, lazy-loving and boozed, in her
red-berried breast. Eyes run from the trees and
windows of the street, steaming 'Gossamer', and strip
her to the nipples and the bees. She blazes naked past
the Sailors Arms, the only woman on the Dai-Adamed
earth. Sinbad Sailors places on her thighs still
dewdamp from the first mangrowing cock-crow
garden his reverent goat-bearded hands.

GOSSAMER BEYNON

I don't care if he *is* common,

SECOND VOICE

she whispers to her salad-day deep self,

GOSSAMER BEYNON

I want to gobble him up. I don't care if he *does* drop his aitches,

SECOND VOICE

she tells the stripped and mother-of-the-world big-beamed and Eve-hipped spring of her self,

GOSSAMER BEYNON

so long as he's all cucumber and hooves.

SECOND VOICE

Sinbad Sailors watches her go by, demure and proud and schoolmarm in her crisp flower dress and sun-defying hat, with never a look or lilt or wriggle, the butcher's unmelting icemaiden daughter veiled for ever from the hungry hug of his eyes.

SINBAD SAILORS

Oh, Gossamer Beynon, why are you so proud?

SECOND VOICE

he grieves to his Guinness,

SINBAD SAILORS

Oh, beautiful beautiful Gossamer B, I wish I wish that you were for me. I wish you were not so educated.

SECOND VOICE

She feels his goatbeard tickle her in the middle of
the world like a tuft of wiry fire, and she turns in a
terror of delight away from his whips and whiskery
conflagration, and sits down in the kitchen to a plate
heaped high with chips and the kidneys of lambs.

FIRST VOICE

In the blind-drawn dark dining-room of School
House, dusty and echoing as a dining-room in a vault,
Mr and Mrs Pugh are silent over cold grey cottage pie.
Mr Pugh reads, as he forks the shroud meat in, from
Lives of the Great Poisoners. He has bound a plain
brown-paper cover round the book. Slyly, between
slow mouthfuls, he sidespies up at Mrs Pugh, poisons
her with his eye, then goes on reading. He underlines
certain passages and smiles in secret.

MRS PUGH

Persons with manners do not read at table,

FIRST VOICE

says Mrs Pugh. She swallows a digestive tablet as big
as a horse-pill, washing it down with clouded peasoup
water.

[*Pause*

MRS PUGH

Some persons were brought up in pigsties.

MR PUGH

Pigs don't read at table, dear.

[65]

FIRST VOICE
> Bitterly she flicks dust from the broken cruet. It
> settles on the pie in a thin gnat-rain.

MR PUGH
> Pigs can't read, my dear.

MRS PUGH
> I know one who can.

FIRST VOICE
> Alone in the hissing laboratory of his wishes, Mr
> Pugh minces among bad vats and jeroboams, tiptoes
> through spinneys of murdering herbs, agony dancing
> in his crucibles, and mixes especially for Mrs Pugh a
> venomous porridge unknown to toxicologists which
> will scald and viper through her until her ears fall
> off like figs, her toes grow big and black as balloons,
> and steam comes screaming out of her navel.

MR PUGH
> You know best, dear,

FIRST VOICE
> says Mr Pugh, and quick as a flash he ducks her in
> rat soup.

MRS PUGH
> What's that book by your trough, Mr Pugh?

MR PUGH
> It's a theological work, my dear. *Lives of the Great
> Saints.*

FIRST VOICE

Mrs Pugh smiles. An icicle forms in the cold air of
the dining-vault.

MRS PUGH

I saw you talking to a saint this morning. Saint
Polly Garter. She was martyred again last night. Mrs
Organ Morgan saw her with Mr Waldo.

MRS ORGAN MORGAN

And when they saw me they pretended they were
looking for nests,

SECOND VOICE

said Mrs Organ Morgan to her husband, with her
mouth full of fish as a pelican's.

MRS ORGAN MORGAN

But you don't go nesting in long combinations, I said
to myself, like Mr Waldo was wearing, and your dress
nearly over your head like Polly Garter's. Oh, they
didn't fool me.

SECOND VOICE

One big bird gulp, and the flounder's gone. She licks
her lips and goes stabbing again.

MRS ORGAN MORGAN

And when you think of all those babies she's got,
then all I can say is she'd better give up bird nesting
that's all I can say, it isn't the right kind of hobby at
all for a woman that can't say No even to midgets.
Remember Bob Spit? He wasn't any bigger than a
baby and he gave her two. But they're two nice boys,

I will say that, Fred Spit and Arthur. Sometimes I
like Fred best and sometimes I like Arthur. Who do
you like best, Organ?

ORGAN MORGAN
　Oh, Bach without any doubt. Bach every time for me.

MRS ORGAN MORGAN
　Organ Morgan, you haven't been listening to a
word I said. It's organ organ all the time with you . . .

FIRST VOICE
　And she bursts into tears, and, in the middle of her
salty howling, nimbly spears a small flatfish and
pelicans it whole.

ORGAN MORGAN
　And then Palestrina,

SECOND VOICE
　says Organ Morgan.

FIRST VOICE
　Lord Cut-Glass, in his kitchen full of time, squats
down alone to a dogdish, marked Fido, of peppery
fish-scraps and listens to the voices of his sixty-six
clocks, one for each year of his loony age, and watches,
with love, their black-and-white moony loudlipped
faces tocking the earth away: slow clocks, quick clocks,
pendulumed heart knocks, china, alarm, grandfather,
cuckoo; clocks shaped like Noah's whirring Ark,
clocks that bicker in marble ships, clocks in the
wombs of glass women, hourglass chimers, tu-wit-tu-
woo clocks, clocks that pluck tunes, Vesuvius clocks
all black bells and lava, Niagara clocks that cataract

their ticks, old time-weeping clocks with ebony beards, clocks with no hands for ever drumming out time without ever knowing what time it is. His sixty-six singers are all set at different hours. Lord Cut-Glass lives in a house and a life at siege. Any minute or dark day now, the unknown enemy will loot and savage downhill, but they will not catch him napping. Sixty-six different times in his fish-slimy kitchen ping, strike, tick, chime, and tock.

SECOND VOICE

The lust and lilt and lather and emerald breeze and crackle of the bird-praise and body of Spring with its breasts full of rivering May-milk, means, to that lordly fish-head nibbler, nothing but another nearness to the tribes and navies of the Last Black Day who'll sear and pillage down Armageddon Hill to his double-locked rusty-shuttered tick-tock dust-scrabbled shack at the bottom of the town that has fallen head over bells in love.

POLLY GARTER

And I'll never have such loving again,

SECOND VOICE

pretty Polly hums and longs.

POLLY GARTER (*Sings*)

Now when farmers' boys on the first fair day
Come down from the hills to drink and be gay,
Before the sun sinks I'll lie there in their arms
For they're *good* bad boys from the lonely farms,
But I always think as we tumble into bed
Of little Willy Wee who is dead, dead, dead . . .

[*A silence*

FIRST VOICE

The sunny slow lulling afternoon yawns and moons
through the dozy town. The sea lolls, laps and idles in,
with fishes sleeping in its lap. The meadows still as
Sunday, the shut-eye tasselled bulls, the goat-and-
daisy dingles, nap happy and lazy. The dumb duck-
ponds snooze. Clouds sag and pillow on Llareggub
Hill. Pigs grunt in a wet wallow-bath, and smile as
they snort and dream. They dream of the acorned
swill of the world, the rooting for pig-fruit, the
bagpipe dugs of the mother sow, the squeal and
snuffle of yesses of the women pigs in rut. They
mud-bask and snout in the pig-loving sun; their tails
curl; they rollick and slobber and snore to deep, smug,
after-swill sleep. Donkeys angelically drowse on
Donkey Down.

MRS PUGH

Persons with manners,

SECOND VOICE

snaps Mrs cold Pugh,

MRS PUGH

do not nod at table.

FIRST VOICE

Mr Pugh cringes awake. He puts on a soft-soaping
smile: it is sad and grey under his nicotine-eggyellow
weeping walrus Victorian moustache worn thick and
long in memory of Doctor Crippen.

MRS PUGH

You should wait until you retire to your sty,

[70]

says Mrs Pugh, sweet as a razor. His fawning
measly quarter-smile freezes. Sly and silent, he foxes
into his chemist's den and there, in a hiss and prussic
circle of cauldrons and phials brimful with pox and
the Black Death, cooks up a fricassee of deadly night-
shade, nicotine, hot frog, cyanide and bat-spit for his
needling stalactite hag and bednag of a pokerbacked
nutcracker wife.

MR PUGH

I beg your pardon, my dear,

SECOND VOICE

he murmurs with a wheedle.

FIRST VOICE

Captain Cat, at his window thrown wide to the sun
and the clippered seas he sailed long ago when his
eyes were blue and bright, slumbers and voyages;
ear-ringed and rolling, I Love You Rosie Probert
tattooed on his belly, he brawls with broken bottles
in the fug and babel of the dark dock bars, roves with
a herd of short and good time cows in every naughty
port and twines and souses with the drowned and
blowzy-breasted dead. He weeps as he sleeps and sails.

SECOND VOICE

One voice of all he remembers most dearly as his
dream buckets down. Lazy early Rosie with the flaxen
thatch, whom he shared with Tom-Fred the donkeyman and many another seaman, clearly and near to
him speaks from the bedroom of her dust. In that
gulf and haven, fleets by the dozen have anchored for

the little heaven of the night; but she speaks to
Captain napping Cat alone. Mrs Probert . . .

ROSIE PROBERT
from Duck Lane, Jack. Quack twice and ask for Rosie

SECOND VOICE
. . . is the one love of his sea-life that was sardined
with women.

ROSIE PROBERT (*Softly*)
What seas did you see,
Tom Cat, Tom Cat,
In your sailoring days
Long long ago?
What sea beasts were
In the wavery green
When you were my master?

CAPTAIN CAT
I'll tell you the truth.
Seas barking like seals,
Blue seas and green,
Seas covered with eels
And mermen and whales.

ROSIE PROBERT
What seas did you sail
Old whaler when
On the blubbery waves
Between Frisco and Wales
You were my bosun?

CAPTAIN CAT

As true as I'm here dear
You Tom Cat's tart
You landlubber Rosie
You cosy love
My easy as easy
My true sweetheart,
Seas green as a bean
Seas gliding with swans
In the seal-barking moon.

ROSIE PROBERT

What seas were rocking
My little deck hand
My favourite husband
In your seaboots and hunger
My duck my whaler
My honey my daddy
My pretty sugar sailor.
With my name on your belly
When you were a boy
Long long ago?

CAPTAIN CAT

I'll tell you no lies.
The only sea I saw
Was the seesaw sea
With you riding on it.
Lie down, lie easy.
Let me shipwreck in your thighs.

ROSIE PROBERT

Knock twice, Jack,
At the door of my grave
And ask for Rosie.

CAPTAIN CAT
    Rosie Probert.

ROSIE PROBERT
    Remember her.
    She is forgetting.
    The earth which filled her mouth
    Is vanishing from her.
    Remember me.
    I have forgotten you.
    I am going into the darkness of the darkness for ever.
    I have forgotten that I was ever born.

CHILD
    Look,

FIRST VOICE
    says a child to her mother as they pass by the window
    of Schooner House,

CHILD
    Captain Cat is crying

FIRST VOICE
    Captain Cat is crying

CAPTAIN CAT
    Come back, come back,

FIRST VOICE
    up the silences and echoes of the passages of the
    eternal night.

CHILD
    He's crying all over his nose.

[74]

FIRST VOICE

says the child. Mother and child move on down the street.

CHILD

He's got a nose like strawberries,

FIRST VOICE

the child says; and then she forgets him too. She sees in the still middle of the bluebagged bay Nogood Boyo fishing from the *Zanzibar*.

CHILD

Nogood Boyo gave me three pennies yesterday but I wouldn't,

FIRST VOICE

the child tells her mother.

SECOND VOICE

Boyo catches a whalebone corset. It is all he has caught all day.

NOGOOD BOYO

Bloody funny fish!

SECOND VOICE

Mrs Dai Bread Two gypsies up his mind's slow eye, dressed only in a bangle.

NOGOOD BOYO

She's wearing her nightgown. (*Pleadingly*) Would you like this nice wet corset, Mrs Dai Bread Two?

MRS DAI BREAD TWO
> No, I *won't*!

NOGOOD BOYO
> And a bite of my little apple?

SECOND VOICE
> he offers with no hope.

FIRST VOICE
> She shakes her brass nightgown, and he chases her out
> of his mind; and when he comes gusting back, there in
> the bloodshot centre of his eye a geisha girl grins
> and bows in a kimono of ricepaper

NOGOOD BOYO
> I want to be *good* Boyo, but nobody'll let me,

FIRST VOICE
> he sighs as she writhes politely. The land fades, the
> sea flocks silently away; and through the warm white
> cloud where he lies, silky, tingling, uneasy Eastern
> music undoes him in a Japanese minute.

SECOND VOICE
> The afternoon buzzes like lazy bees round the flowers
> round Mae Rose Cottage. Nearly asleep in the field of
> nannygoats who hum and gently butt the sun, she
> blows love on a puffball.

MAE ROSE COTTAGE (*Lazily*)
> He loves me
> He loves me not
> He loves me
> He loves me not
> He *loves* me! – the dirty old fool.

[76]

Lazy she lies alone in clover and sweet-grass,
seventeen and never been sweet in the grass ho ho.

FIRST VOICE
The Reverend Eli Jenkins inky in his cool front
parlour or poem-room tells only the truth in his
Lifework – the Population, Main Industry, Shipping,
History, Topography, Flora and Fauna of the town he
worships in – the White Book of Llareggub. Portraits
of famous bards and preachers, all fur and wool from
the squint to the kneecaps, hang over him heavy as
sheep, next to faint lady watercolours of pale green
Milk Wood like a lettuce salad dying. His mother,
propped against a pot in a palm, with her wedding-
ring waist and bust like a black-clothed dining-table
suffers in her stays.

REV. ELI JENKINS
Oh angels be careful there with your knives and forks,

FIRST VOICE
he prays. There is no known likeness of his father
Esau, who, undogcollared because of his little
weakness, was scythed to the bone one harvest by
mistake when sleeping with his weakness in the corn.
He lost all ambition and died, with one leg.

REV. ELI JENKINS
Poor Dad,

SECOND VOICE
grieves the Reverend Eli,

REV. ELI JENKINS
  to die of drink and agriculture.

SECOND VOICE
  Farmer Watkins in Salt Lake Farm hates his cattle
  on the hill as he ho's them in to milking.

UTAH WATKINS (*In a fury*)
  Damn you, you damned dairies!

SECOND VOICE
  A cow kisses him.

UTAH WATKINS
  Bite her to death!

SECOND VOICE
  he shouts to his deaf dog who smiles and licks his
  hands.

UTAH WATKINS
  Gore him, sit on him, Daisy!

SECOND VOICE
  he bawls to the cow who barbed him with her tongue,
  and she moos gentle words as he raves and dances
  among his summerbreathed slaves walking delicately
  to the farm. The coming of the end of the Spring
  day is already reflected in the lakes of their great eyes.
  Bessie Bighead greets them by the names she gave
  them when they were maidens.

[78]

BESSIE BIGHEAD
Peg, Meg, Buttercup, Moll,
Fan from the Castle,
Theodosia and Daisy.

SECOND VOICE
They bow their heads.

FIRST VOICE
Look up Bessie Bighead in the White Book of
Llareggub and you will find the few haggard rags and
the one poor glittering thread of her history laid out in
pages there with as much love and care as the lock of
hair of a first lost love. Conceived in Milk Wood, born
in a barn, wrapped in paper, left on a doorstep,
big-headed and bass-voiced she grew in the dark until
long-dead Gomer Owen kissed her when she wasn't
looking because he was dared. Now in the light she'll
work, sing, milk, say the cows' sweet names and sleep
until the night sucks out her soul and spits it into the
sky. In her life-long love light, holily Bessie milks the
fond lake-eyed cows as dusk showers slowly down
over byre, sea and town. Utah Watkins curses through
the farmyard on a carthorse.

UTAH WATKINS
Gallop, you bleeding cripple!

FIRST VOICE
and the huge horse neighs softly as though he had
given it a lump of sugar.
    Now the town is dusk. Each cobble, donkey, goose
and gooseberry street is a thoroughfare of dusk; and
dusk and ceremonial dust, and night's first darkening

[79]

snow, and the sleep of birds, drift under and through the live dusk of this place of love. Llareggub is the capital of dusk.

Mrs Ogmore-Pritchard, at the first drop of the dusk-shower, seals all her sea-view doors, draws the germ-free blinds, sits, erect as a dry dream on a high-backed hygienic chair and wills herself to cold, quick sleep. At once, at twice, Mr Ogmore and Mr Pritchard, who all dead day long have been gossiping like ghosts in the woodshed, planning the loveless destruction of their glass widow, reluctantly sigh and sidle into her clean house.

MR PRITCHARD
You first, Mr Ogmore.

MR OGMORE
After you, Mr Pritchard.

MR PRITCHARD
No, no, Mr Ogmore. You widowed her first.

FIRST VOICE
And in through the keyhole, with tears where their eyes once were, they ooze and grumble.

MRS OGMORE-PRITCHARD
Husbands,

FIRST VOICE
she says in her sleep. There is acid love in her voice for one of the two shambling phantoms. Mr Ogmore hopes that it is not for him. So does Mr Pritchard.

MRS OGMORE-PRITCHARD
I love you both.

MR OGMORE (*With terror*)
Oh, Mrs Ogmore.

MR PRITCHARD (*With horror*)
Oh, Mrs Pritchard.

MRS OGMORE-PRITCHARD
Soon it will be time to go to bed. Tell me your tasks in order.

MR OGMORE AND MR PRITCHARD
We must take our pyjamas from the drawer marked pyjamas.

MRS OGMORE-PRITCHARD (*Coldly*)
And then you must take them off.

SECOND VOICE
Down in the dusking town, Mae Rose Cottage, still lying in clover, listens to the nannygoats chew, draws circles of lipstick round her nipples.

MAE ROSE COTTAGE
I'm *fast*. I'm a bad lot. God will strike me dead. I'm seventeen. I'll go to hell,

SECOND VOICE
she tells the goats.

MAE ROSE COTTAGE
You just wait. I'll sin till I blow up!

SECOND VOICE
> She lies deep, waiting for the worst to happen; the
> goats champ and sneer.

FIRST VOICE
> And at the doorway of Bethesda House, the Reverend
> Jenkins recites to Llareggub Hill his sunset poem.

REV. ELI JENKINS
> Every morning when I wake,
> Dear Lord, a little prayer I make,
> O please to keep Thy lovely eye
> On all poor creatures born to die.
>
> And every evening at sun-down
> I ask a blessing on the town,
> For whether we last the night or no
> I'm sure is always touch-and-go.
>
> We are not wholly bad or good
> Who live our lives under Milk Wood,
> And Thou, I know, wilt be the first
> To see our best side, not our worst.
>
> O let us see another day!
> Bless us all this night, I pray,
> And to the sun we all will bow
> And say, good-bye – but just for now!

FIRST VOICE
> Jack Black prepares once more to meet his Satan in the
> Wood. He grinds his night-teeth, closes his eyes,
> climbs into his religious trousers, their flies sewn up
> with cobbler's thread, and pads out, torched and
> bibled, grimly, joyfully, into the already sinning dusk.

[82]

JACK BLACK

Off to Gomorrah!

SECOND VOICE

And Lily Smalls is up to Nogood Boyo in the wash-house.

FIRST VOICE

And Cherry Owen, sober as Sunday as he is every day of the week, goes off happy as Saturday to get drunk as a deacon as he does every night.

CHERRY OWEN

I always say she's got two husbands.

FIRST VOICE

says Cherry Owen,

CHERRY OWEN

one drunk and one sober.

FIRST VOICE

And Mrs Cherry simply says

MRS CHERRY OWEN

And aren't I a lucky woman? Because I love them both.

SINBAD

Evening, Cherry.

CHERRY OWEN

Evening, Sinbad.

SINBAD
What'll you have?

CHERRY OWEN
Too much.

SINBAD
The Sailors Arms is always open . . .

FIRST VOICE
Sinbad suffers to himself, heartbroken,

SINBAD
. . . oh, Gossamer, open yours!

FIRST VOICE
Dusk is drowned for ever until to-morrow. It is all at
once night now. The windy town is a hill of windows,
and from the larrupped waves the lights of the lamps
in the windows call back the day and the dead that
have run away to sea. All over the calling dark, babies
and old men are bribed and lullabied to sleep.

FIRST WOMAN'S VOICE
Hushabye, baby, the sandman is coming . . .

SECOND WOMAN'S VOICE (*Singing*)
Rockabye, grandpa, in the tree top,
When the wind blows the cradle will rock,
When the bough breaks the cradle will fall,
Down will come grandpa, whiskers and all.

FIRST VOICE
Or their daughters cover up the old unwinking men

like parrots, and in their little dark in the lit and
bustling young kitchen corners, all night long they
watch, beady-eyed, the long night through in case
death catches them asleep.

SECOND VOICE
Unmarried girls, alone in their privately bridal
bedrooms, powder and curl for the Dance of the
World.
[*Accordion music: dim*
They make, in front of their looking-glasses,
haughty or come-hithering faces for the young men
in the street outside, at the lamplit leaning corners,
who wait in the all-at-once wind to wolve and whistle.
[*Accordion music louder, then fading under*

FIRST VOICE
The drinkers in the Sailors Arms drink to the failure
of the dance.

A DRINKER
Down with the waltzing and the skipping.

CHERRY OWEN
Dancing isn't natural,

FIRST VOICE
righteously says Cherry Owen who has just downed
seventeen pints of flat, warm, thin, Welsh, bitter beer.

SECOND VOICE
A farmer's lantern glimmers, a spark on Llareggub
hillside.
[*Accordion music fades into silence*

FIRST VOICE
Llareggub Hill, writes the Reverend Jenkins in his poem-room,

REV. ELI JENKINS
Llareggub Hill, that mystic tumulus, the memorial of peoples that dwelt in the region of Llareggub before the Celts left the Land of Summer and where the old wizards made themselves a wife out of flowers.

SECOND VOICE
Mr Waldo, in his corner of the Sailors Arms, sings:

MR WALDO
In Pembroke City when I was young
I lived by the Castle Keep
Sixpence a week was my wages
For working for the chimbley-sweep.
Six cold pennies he gave me
Not a farthing more or less
And all the fare I could afford
Was parsnip gin and watercress.
I did not need a knife and fork
Or a bib up to my chin.
To dine on a dish of watercress
And a jug of parsnip gin.
Did you ever hear a growing boy
To live so cruel cheap
On grub that has no flesh and bones
And liquor that makes you weep?
Sweep sweep chimbley sweep,
I wept through Pembroke City
Poor and barefoot in the snow
Till a kind young woman took pity.

Poor little chimbley sweep she said
Black as the ace of spades
O nobody's swept my chimbley
Since my husband went his ways.
Come and sweep my chimbley
Come and sweep my chimbley
She sighed to me with a blush
Come and sweep my chimbley
Come and sweep my chimbley
Bring along your chimbley brush!

FIRST VOICE
Blind Captain Cat climbs into his bunk. Like a cat,
he sees in the dark. Through the voyages of his tears
he sails to see the dead.

CAPTAIN CAT
Dancing Williams!

FIRST DROWNED
Still dancing.

CAPTAIN CAT
Jonah Jarvis.

THIRD DROWNED
Still.

FIRST DROWNED
Curly Bevan's skull.

ROSIE PROBERT
Rosie, with God. She has forgotten dying.

FIRST VOICE

The dead come out in their Sunday best.

SECOND VOICE

Listen to the night breaking.

FIRST VOICE

Organ Morgan goes to chapel to play the organ. He
sees Bach lying on a tombstone.

ORGAN MORGAN

Johann Sebastian!

CHERRY OWEN (*Drunkenly*)

Who?

ORGAN MORGAN

Johann Sebastian mighty Bach. Oh, Bach fach.

CHERRY OWEN

To hell with you,

FIRST VOICE

says Cherry Owen who is resting on the tombstone on
his way home.

Mr Mog Edwards and Miss Myfanwy Price happily
apart from one another at the top and the sea end of
the town write their everynight letters of love and
desire. In the warm White Book of Llareggub you will
find the little maps of the islands of their contentment.

MYFANWY PRICE

Oh, my Mog, I am yours for ever.

FIRST VOICE

And she looks around with pleasure at her own neat neverdull room which Mr Mog Edwards will never enter.

MOG EDWARDS

Come to my arms, Myfanwy.

FIRST VOICE

And he hugs his lovely money to his *own* heart.

And Mr Waldo drunk in the dusky wood hugs his lovely Polly Garter under the eyes and rattling tongues of the neighbours and the birds, and he does not care. He smacks his live red lips.

But it is not *his* name that Polly Garter whispers as she lies under the oak and loves him back. Six feet deep that name sings in the cold earth.

POLLY GARTER (*Sings*)

But I always think as we tumble into bed
Of little Willy Wee who is dead, dead, dead.

FIRST VOICE

The thin night darkens. A breeze from the creased water sighs the streets close under Milk waking Wood. The Wood, whose every tree-foot's cloven in the black glad sight of the hunters of lovers, that is a God-built garden to Mary Ann Sailors who knows there is a Heaven on earth and the chosen people of His kind fire in Llareggub's land, that is the fairday farmhands' wantoning ignorant chapel of bridesbeds, and, to the Reverend Eli Jenkins, a greenleaved sermon on the innocence of men, the suddenly wind-shaken wood springs awake for the second dark time this one Spring day.

[89]

Notes on Pronunciation

[Page 2] *Rhiannon:* strongly aspirated *r*, and accent on the
second syllable. *Llareggub:* a voiceless *l* produced from
the side of the mouth, accent on the second syllable, the
third syllable rhyming with 'bib'. *Dai:* as 'dye'.

[Page 6] *Dowlais:* accent on the first syllable, the second
syllable rhyming with 'ice'. *Maesgwyn:* mice-gwin,
accent on the second syllable.

[Page 7] *Myfanwy:* accent on the second syllable, *f* as *v*, the
first *y* an indeterminate sound, the second *y* as *ee*.

[Page 8] *Ach y fi:* the *ch* guttural, the *y* indeterminate, *f* as
v, the whole pronounced as one word; an interjection
expressing disgust.

[Page 13] *mwchins:* a compromise between the English
'mooching' and the Welsh dialect word 'mitching',
playing truant.

[Page 21] *Eisteddfodau:* eye-steth-vod-eye, the *th* voiced, a
strong accent on the third syllable.

[Page 22] *Parchs:* the *ch* gutteral; clergymen. *Organ
Morgan:* the *r*'s rolled, the *o*'s short.

[Page 23] *Gippo:* gypsy.

[Page 25] *Dewi:* de-wee, the first syllable, which has the accent, is short.

[Page 26] *Moel yr Wyddfa:* moil-er-ooithva, the *th* voiced. *Carnedd:* the *dd* a voiced *th*, the *r* rolled, accent on the first syllable. *Penmaenmawr:* 'maen' rhymes with 'line', 'mawr' with 'hour'. *Sawdde:* southay, the *th* voiced. *Edw:* aid-oo. *Llyfnant:* *y* indeterminate, *f* as *v*. *Claerwen, Cleddau, Dulais:* clir-wen; cleth-eye, the *th* voiced: dill-ice. *Ogwr:* ogoorr, accent on the first syllable. *Cennen:* the *c* hard.

[Page 40] *Gerwain:* Gerr-wine, the *g* hard. *Ty:* as 'tee'.

[Page 42] *Gorslas:* gorse-lahss, with a strong accent on the second syllable.

[Page 51] *Twll:* ooll, the *oo* short, the *ll* as in 'Llareggub'.

[Page 63] *cawl:* as 'cowl': a broth with leeks.

[Page 88] *fach:* an expression of endearment; *f* as *v*, and the *ch* guttural.

FIRST BROADCAST

FULL CAST

First Voice	*Richard Burton*
Second Voice	*Richard Bebb*
Captain Cat	*Hugh Griffith*
First Drowned	*Dillwyn Owen*
Second Drowned	*Meredith Edwards*
Rosie Probert	*Rachel Thomas*
Third Drowned	*John Huw Jones*
Fourth Drowned	*Philip Burton*
Fifth Drowned	*John Ormond Thomas*
Mr Mog Edwards	*Dafydd Havard*
Miss Myfanwy Price . . .	*Sybil Williams*
Jack Black	*John Glyn Jones*
Waldo's Mother	*Olwen Brookes*
Little Boy Waldo	*Diana Maddox*
Waldo's Wife	*Mary Jones*
Mr Waldo	*Meredith Edwards*
First Neighbour	*Dilys Davies*
Second Neighbour	*Rachel Roberts*
Third Neighbour	*Lorna Davies*
Fourth Neighbour	*Gwenllian Owen*
Matti's Mother	*Rachel Thomas*
First Woman	*Rachel Roberts*
Second Woman	*Sybil Williams*
Third Woman	*Gwyneth Petty*
Fourth Woman	*Olwen Brookes*
Fifth Woman	*Lorna Davies*
Preacher	*Philip Burton*
Mrs Ogmore-Pritchard . . .	*Dilys Davies*
Mr Ogmore	*David Close-Thomas*
Mr Pritchard	*Ben Williams*
Gossamer Beynon	*Gwenllian Owen*
Organ Morgan	*John Glyn Jones*
Utah Watkins	*Meredith Edwards*
Mrs Utah Watkins	*Rachel Thomas*
Ocky Milkman	*Dillwyn Owen*
A Voice	*John Huw Jones*

Mrs Willy Nilly	. . . . .	Rachel Thomas
Lily Smalls	. . . . .	Gwyneth Petty
Mae Rose Cottage	. . . .	Rachel Roberts
Butcher Beynon	. . . .	Meredith Edwards
Rev. Eli Jenkins	. . . .	Philip Burton
Mr Pugh	. . . . .	John Huw Jones
Mrs Organ Morgan	. . . .	Olwen Brookes
Mary Ann Sailors	. . . .	Rachel Thomas
Dai Bread	. . . . .	David Close-Thomas
Polly Garter	. . . . .	Diana Maddox
Nogood Boyo	. . . .	Dillwyn Owen
Lord Cut-Glass	. . . .	John Glyn Jones
Gwennie	. . . . .	Norma Jones
Mrs Beynon	. . . . .	Olwen Brookes
Mrs Pugh	. . . . .	Mary Jones
Mrs Dai Bread One	. . . .	Gwyneth Petty
Mrs Dai Bread Two	. . . .	Rachel Roberts
Willy Nilly	. . . . .	Ben Williams
Mrs Cherry Owen	. . . .	Lorna Davies
Cherry Owen	. . . . .	John Ormond Thomas
Sinbad	. . . . .	Aubrey Richards
Old Man	. . . . .	David Close-Thomas
First Neighbour	. . . .	Gwyneth Petty
Second Neighbour	. . . .	Sybil Williams
Third Neighbour	. . . .	Lorna Davies
Fourth Neighbour	. . . .	Mary Jones
Evans the Death	. . . .	Meredith Edwards
Fisherman	. . . . .	Dillwyn Owen
Child	. . . . .	Norma Jones
Bessie Bighead	. . . .	Gwyneth Petty
First Woman	. . . . .	Gwenllian Owen
Second Woman	. . . .	Rachel Roberts
A Drinker	. . . . .	Dafydd Havard

Children of Laugharne School, Carmarthenshire

Everyman
A selection of titles

* indicates volumes available in paperback

Complete lists of Everyman's Library and Everyman Paperbacks
are available from the Sales Department, J.M. Dent and Sons
Ltd, 91 Clapham High Street, London SW4 7TA

ESSAYS AND CRITICISM

*Bacon, Francis. *Essays*
*Coleridge, Samuel Taylor. *Biographia Literaria*
*Emerson, Ralph. *Essays*
*Jerome, Jerome K. *Idle Thoughts of an Idle Fellow*
*Milton. John. *Prose Writings*
 Montaigne, Michael Eyquem de. *Essays* (3 vols)
 Spencer, Herbert. *Essays on Education and Kindred Subjects*
*Swift, Jonathan. *Tale of a Tub and other satires*

HISTORY

**The Anglo-Saxon Chronicle*
**Autobiography of Richard Baxter*
 Bede. *Ecclesiastical History of the English Nation*
*Burnet, Gilbert. *History of His Own Time*
 Geoffrey of Monmouth. *History of the Kings of Britain*
 Gibbon, Edward. *The Decline and Fall of the Roman Empire*
        (6 vols)
*Hollingshead, John. *Ragged London in 1861*
 Prescott, W.H. *History of the Conquest of Mexico*
*Stow, John. *The Survey of London*
 Voltaire. *The Age of Louis XIV*
*Woodhouse, A.S.P. *Puritanism and Liberty*

LEGENDS AND SAGAS

* *Beowulf and Its Analogues*
* Chrétien de Troyes. *Arthurian Romances*
* *Egils saga*
* *Kudrun*
* *The Mabinogin*
* *The Saga of Gisli*
* *The Saga of Grettir the Strong*
* Snorri Sturluson. *Edda*
* Wace and Layamon. *Arthurian Chronicles*

POETRY AND DRAMA

* *Anglo-Saxon Poetry*
* Arnold, Matthew. *Selected Poems and Prose*
* Blake, William. *Selected Poems*
* Brontës, The. *Selected Poems*
* Browning, Robert. *Men and Women and other poems*
* Burns, Robert. *The Kilmarnock Poems*
* Chaucer, Geoffrey, *Canterbury Tales*
* Clare, John. *Selected Poems*
* Coleridge, Samuel Taylor. *Poems*
* Donne, John. *The Complete English Poems*
* *Elizabethan Sonnets*
* *English Moral Interludes*
* *Everyman and Medieval Miracle Plays*
* *Everyman's Book of Evergreen Verse*
* *Everyman's Book of Victorian Verse*
* Gay, John. *The Beggar's Opera and other eighteenth-century plays*
* *The Golden Treasury of Longer Poems*
* Hardy, Thomas. *Selected Poems*
* Herbert, George. *The English Poems*
* Hopkins, Gerard Manley. *The Major Poems*
  Ibsen, Henrik
    * *A Doll's House; The Wild Duck; The Lady from the Sea*
    * *Hedda Gabler; The Master Builder; John Gabriel Borkman*
* Keats, John. *Poems*

*Langland, William. *The Vision of Piers Plowman*
*Longfellow, Henry. *Poems*
*Marlowe, Christopher. *Complete Plays and Poems*
*Marvell, Andrew. *Complete Poetry*
*Middleton, Thomas. *Three Plays*
*Milton, John. *Complete Poems*
Palgrave's Golden Treasury
Pearl, Cleanness, Patience and *Sir Gawain and the Green
     Knight*
Poems of the Second World War
*Pope, Alexander. *Collected Poems*
The Ramayana and Mahábhárata
Restoration Plays
The Rubáiyát of Omar Khayyám and other Persian poems
*Shelley, Percy Bysshe. *Selected Poems*
Silver Poets of the 16th Century
Six Middle English Romances
*Spenser, Edmund. *The Faerie Queene: Books I to III*
The Stuffed Owl
*Synge, J.M. *Plays, Poems and Prose*
*Tennyson, Alfred. *In Memoriam, Maud and other poems*
Thomas, Dylan
     Collected Poems, 1934–1952
     The Poems
     Under Milk Wood
*Webster and Ford. *Selected Plays*
*Wilde, Oscar. *Plays, Prose Writings and Poems*
*Wordsworth, William. *Selected Poems*

RELIGION AND PHILOSOPHY

---

*Bacon, Francis. *The Advancement of Learning*
*Berkeley, George. *Philosophical Works*
The Buddha's Philosophy of Man
*Carlyle, Thomas. *Sartor Resartus*
Chinese Philosophy in Classical Times
*Descartes, René. *A Discourse on Method*
Hindu Scriptures
*Hobbes, Thomas. *Leviathan*
*Kant, Immanuel. *A Critique of Pure Reason*

*The Koran
*Leibniz, Gottfried Wilhelm. *Philosophical Writings*
*Locke, John. *An Essay Concerning Human Understanding (abridgement)*
*More, Thomas. *Utopia*
Pascal, Blaise. *Pensées*
Plato. *The Trial and Death of Socrates*
*Spinoza, Benedictus de. *Ethics*

SCIENCES: POLITICAL AND GENERAL

Coleridge, Samuel Taylor. *On the Constitution of the Church and State*
Derry, John. *English Politics and the American Revolution*
Harvey, William. *The Circulation of the Blood and other writings*
*Locke, John. *Two Treatises of Government*
*Machiavelli, Niccolò. *The Prince and other political writings*
*Malthus, Thomas. *An Essay on the Principle of Population*
*Mill, J.S. *Utilitarianism; On Liberty: Representative Government*
*Plato. *The Republic*
*Ricardo, David. *Principles of Political Economy and Taxation*
Rousseau, J.-J.
    Emile
    The Social Contract and *Discourses*
*Wollstonecraft, Mary. *A Vindication of the Rights of Woman*

TRAVEL AND TOPOGRAPHY

Boswell, James. *The Journal of a Tour to the Hebrides*
Darwin, Charles. *The Voyage of the 'Beagle'*
*Hudson, W.H. *Idle Days in Patagonia*
*Kingsley, Mary. *Travels in West Africa*
*Stevenson, R.L. *An Inland Voyage; Travels with a Donkey; The Silverado Squatters*
*Thomas, Edward. *The South Country*
Travels of Marco Polo
*White, Gilbert. *The Natural History of Selborne*